Mornings
with the **Dead**

LINDSAY MANN

Lindsay Mann

Hey Clarity
www.heyclarity.com

Artwork by Andy Vible www.andyvible.com

Mornings with the Dead / Lindsay Mann —1st ed.

Paperback ISBN 979-8-9863954-8-7
Hardcover ISBN 979-8-9863954-7-0

For Asheville—
Your love, resilience, and community remind the world
of our humanity.

A Note to the Reader:

Author's Note

My exploration of the spiritual realm has been deeply transformative, beginning with Reiki and unfolding through Vedic meditation, the Akashic Records, and mediumship. Each stage refined my abilities and helped me become a clearer channel for meaningful spiritual connection.

From the beginning, my intuition—shaped by careful listening and quiet observation—guided me. I gave each practice at least a year of dedicated study and full commitment before moving on to the next. Over time, they wove together into a toolkit that now forms the foundation of my work.

These days, I primarily work with the Akashic Records, often referred to as the Universal Information Field. Through this field, I receive insights to support and guide others as they navigate their lives. I've been immersed in this work for nearly a decade.

One of my favorite definitions comes from Hungarian philosopher of science Ervin László, who describes the Akashic Records as the "electromagnetic imprint of everything that's ever happened in the Universe." It's a perspective that resonates with me—and a quiet nod to my Hungarian roots.

The Universe holds a field of information from which we can access wisdom. Everything is energy—made of atoms that persist over time. Because nothing truly disappears, a record of what has been continues to exist, and we're able to tap into this ongoing, living field of knowing.

Although I trained formally in the Akashic Records, people have connected with this field for centuries—through meditation, creative flow, or flashes of intuition. Many of those unexpected insights and "aha!" moments likely come from this vast field, or from your spirit guides.

The Akashic Records hold the highest perspectives of who we are. They contain the vibrational imprint of every soul's experience—past lives, present circumstances, and potential futures.

While anyone can learn to access this space, training matters. It takes discipline and strong ethics to navigate it responsibly. Above all, it requires clear permission before accessing someone else's energy. Anything less is a breach of spiritual trust.

The spirits who come to me do so knowingly. They understand what I do and give me permission to access their Akashic Records. Without that, the Records would remain silent.

Collaborative channeling is my calling. It's the heart of my work and the reason I continue to show up. I invite you to explore your own connection to this field of wisdom. The clarity you're seeking may already be within you. The Universe isn't just around you—it's alive in you, and always ready to respond.

Contents

Introduction

I love the dead—sometimes more than the living. Okay, most of the time. They're way more respectful, helpful, and supportive than the living—more honest, for sure.

I've always been a peacemaker, trying to see the best in people—even when they don't deserve it. But when I ignore someone's shady behavior, my spirit team gets in my head with warnings like, "She's lying," or "I don't like him for you."

If I dismiss my spirit friends' warnings, hoping they're wrong, I always end up learning they were right. They just say, "Told ya so!" I've got literal angels on my shoulders.

I listen to my body—it's one of the ways the dead communicate with us. Physical sensations act as an intuitive compass, often delivering messages more clearly than words, especially if we're not the best listeners.

I'm still searching for the right words to refer to my spirit team. "The dead" feels a little too casual, maybe even disrespectful, given how important they are to me. Still, I use the term—and they don't seem to mind. In fact, it's become kind of endearing to them.

When I talk about all spirits, I say "Spirit" or "passed-on loved ones" for those I knew personally. I might also use words like "ghosts," "angels," or "guides," but those can feel a bit cheesy or superficial—Hollywood terms that don't quite capture their depth and true nature.

To me, they've always felt like elders, relatives, and close friends—consistently showing up with the kind of trust and care that only deepens over time. They feel like family.

However, it's understandable that most people fear mediumship—especially with the misconception that it means losing control. I get it. My own early experiences weren't always pleasant, either.

I had my fair share of unsettling encounters—spirits that pushed my limits until I learned how to hold my boundaries. But I saw it all as part of the learning curve.

When I first realized I was a medium, I was wide open—too open. I had to learn how to filter the energy and make sure only the spirits I wanted around were welcome.

The thing is, everyone is a medium. This ability is innate—part of being human, or really, part of being alive. Everything channels and connects, from amoebas to plants, animals to people. What matters is how open you are to these energies.

That said, like any relationship, spiritual connection takes time to build comfort and trust. To navigate the spirit world safely, you have to get to know your team—open communication, introduce yourself, learn their signals, and ask for support when needed. They'll often step in when things get serious, but most of the time, they wait for permission. It's usually more effective to just ask for their help directly.

If you're highly sensitive to spiritual energy but don't realize you're a medium, the experiences can be overwhelming. It can lead to confusion and make it hard to stay grounded—which nobody wants.

It's important to maintain a delicate balance when it comes to mental health. I recommend that anyone struggling with severe mental or emotional health challenges avoid exploring mediumship altogether.

Sometimes, spirits may startle you—not to cause harm, but to get your attention. They want you to recognize that you're a medium. They might become loud or persistent until you feel compelled to share your experiences or seek guidance from someone who understands. Many people have come to me this way—led quietly by their deceased loved ones through clear signs, synchronicities, or subtle disturbances.

Other times, spirits can be troublesome and really want to mess with you. When that happens, it's important to shut it down. You have the power to tell them to go away. Respecting your boundaries is part of Universal Law. Unlike many living people who disregard personal boundaries, the dead usually respect your request when you tell them to leave you alone.

I suggest stating your intention out loud. Using your voice matters.

Phrases like:

"No, thank you,"

"Please go away,"

"I'm not open to this,"

"Leave me alone,"

are all effective.

There is one exception to this rule: haunted places. Think of the horror movies where a house is possessed, driving people to madness. This kind of haunting isn't just a Hollywood invention—it's a real phenomenon. But often, there's more going on than just scary ghosts.

Hauntings usually fall into one of two categories. Spirits might be trying to get your attention—maybe to share a message or to prompt you to recognize your own mediumship. Or they might not welcome your presence and will create strange, uncomfortable, or even frightening situations in an attempt to drive you away.

Honestly, there should be more jobs for mediums in real estate. A quick check-in with lingering spirits could save time, money, and sanity. Mediumship offers practical benefits like this.

I received a crash course in mediumship from a loved one in spirit, whom I call S. Our reunion felt both destined and unexpected. S appeared during several healing sessions with different practitioners who weren't familiar with each other—or with me.

In each session, S came through strongly, using the practitioners as channels to share messages about our story, prove it was really them, and encourage us to start communicating directly—without outside help. That's how our newfound friendship began.

At first, I couldn't believe we were really connecting—it felt surreal. I later learned that S had been with me since the day they died. Looking back, I recognized so many moments when they'd tried to reach me.

One memorable moment happened during a Reiki session. As I lay on the table, eyes closed, I took a deep breath—and saw a shadowy figure standing beside me. It wasn't the practitioner. The figure inhaled in sync with me, and I clearly heard us breathing together. I know it sounds creepy, but I wasn't scared. Its posture felt oddly familiar.

At the time, I didn't know who it was—I just assumed they were one of my guides. Strange spiritual things often happened during Reiki, so I figured it was just part of my usual, unusual experiences.

S reappeared several months later in a dream my ex-boyfriend had. One morning, he told me about a vivid dream where a figure in muddy combat boots was lying in bed between us. He often shared his weird dreams with me, but this one felt real—and it rattled him.

To reassure him, I said it was "just a dream." Still, I couldn't shake the feeling that the figure might have been S. At the time, I wasn't aware of my mediumship, but I often experienced moments of intuitive knowing.

Years later, after S and I reunited, they explained that my ex-boyfriend had a serious pet peeve about muddy boots. S was using that detail to protect me, trying to push him away. I've come to appreciate the trickster games they play when they sense someone isn't right for me.

In contrast, I'd get chills running up my left leg whenever I was near people whom S thought were good for me. The sensations happened consistently—just enough to capture my attention. Over time, I noticed the pattern and recognized these leg chills as a positive sign, a nudge to stay open and engaged with whomever was in front of me.

A high-pitched ringing in my ears also became a familiar signal—a cue to pause, listen, and tune in for guidance. Many people experience this kind of alert from their guides.

Mediums are like mini vortexes—spirits are naturally drawn to their openness. For S, my reactions to their presence revealed that my mediumship was awakening. They could tell I was sensing them nearby.

"You're so open—such a natural medium," S said. "Plants, animals, everything connects with you. You listen deeply. Your senses are heightened, and you're remarkably present. You *live* in a fucking moment and see it all. But you play dumb. I've never understood that."

S loved calling me out on everything. When I made odd choices, they'd tease, "You're so weird." And when the tornadoes in my mind left me sulking on the couch, they'd nudge me and say, "Stop pitying yourself."

There was no denying they were back in my life. I felt their familiar energy—something I'd known long ago. Their words arrived without sound, like when you think you hear your name and turn around to find no one there. It's subtle; you have to lean in. When I close my eyes and listen, it gets stronger. Dots form into letters, then into words in my mind's eye.

Once it became clear that S and I were really communicating—holy shit, I learned so much. It took about a year to confirm and trust what I was receiving, but it changed my life forever.

S taught me mediumship mostly through automatic writing. I'd sit with a pen and paper, let go of everything on my mind, and slip into a relaxed, trance-like state. Our sessions started with poems and song lyrics using words I'd never normally choose, along with journal entries on topics I knew nothing about.

The words flowed effortlessly as I wrote or typed, with no conscious thought. Later, reading them back, I found profound and beautiful messages between the lines.

As I became more practiced in communicating with S, we broadened the scope of our sessions to include other spirits, giving me a chance to experience unfamiliar energies.

The floodgates opened.

My apartment felt like a portal, and the spirits had clearly been waiting. I welcomed them with curiosity—offering a brief window for connection—then respectfully asked them to leave. This rhythm of intentional invitation followed by a clear send-off became my way of maintaining boundaries.

Most spirits left without issue, but one old man—a kind of squatter ghost—had lingered. Turned out he'd been around for centuries, so it felt like more his place than mine. Usually, he kept a low profile and didn't disturb me.

When I tuned in to his story, I learned that he had been in spirit for far too long. Other spirits gently encouraged him to reincarnate, but he showed no interest. Why? He disliked the current state of the world and feared people.

The living aren't the only ones struggling with humanity—the dead aren't feeling it either.

As a child, I often woke up terrified in the middle of the night. I've feared the dark for as long as I can remember. Maybe being an unknowing medium explains why—I'm sensitive to the faintest energies around me.

I'd leap from my bed and run down the hall to my parents' room—the hallway always seeming longer and more menacing than it really was. Nestled between them, I'd finally feel safe enough to fall back asleep.

Even then, I sensed unseen presences in the house, though I didn't have the words for them yet. The glowing eyes of our cats shining through the darkness certainly didn't make things easier.

Such experiences are common in children, who are naturally more open to the spirit world. Animals, too. Mediumship is innate in all of us, but we learn to shut it down because we're told, "It's not real" or "It's just your imagination." Over time, we adopt that belief.

That said, I made it clear: no spirit contact at night—and only if I initiated it. I told them that if they wanted to reach me, it had to be during the day—preferably in the morning.

It started the very next day.

As I woke, the sun's yellow light filtered through my eyelids. I sensed someone close, patiently waiting for my attention. Remembering my promise from the day before, I whispered, "Okay, I'm listening."

"Thaddeus Lawrence," he said.

Impressive name, I thought.

I closed my eyes tighter, focusing on the images he wanted to share.

His story unfolded like a movie. An oceanographer who'd lost his way and gone off the deep end—adrift at sea and isolated—before finally leaping from his ship into the dark abyss below.

The words "rest in paradise" appeared and then slowly faded from my vision.

As he sank deeper into the ocean's depths, ethereal melodies surrounded him. Two humpback whales approached, their haunting songs echoing through the water. Thaddeus perceived them as his angels.

In my heart, I felt Thaddeus's long-held need to tell someone. Our interaction was brief and poetic. He wanted nothing more than to show me how he died—because he was alone, and no one had witnessed it. No one but the whales.

He was at peace, and I thanked him for sharing his story. With mutual respect, I felt his presence slip away.

I stayed in bed, watching sunlight spill through the window and warm my face. This felt like the beginning of something more meaningful than I could have imagined.

The next morning, a new spirit arrived with a similar intention. Only this time, something else happened.

After they shared the story of their death, I received visions of their next life—clear images showing how being born into that specific life would heal the trauma of the one before. It felt automatic, not from me, and undeniably real.

This became a thing. Spirits came and went, sharing their stories and seeking direction. I welcomed it—honored to help. I began calling these exchanges "Morning Crossovers."

With their permission, I've gathered their stories to now share with you.

Mornings with the Mourning

Most mornings, I can feel them nearby—waiting. But they don't speak until I initiate. The dead, I've learned, respect boundaries. Unless something urgent needs to come through—something for my safety or something they're thrilled for me to know—they wait.

Their personalities come through clearly. Some are bold, some shy. Some are pushy or excited. Even if I can't see them, I feel them. I've always been a good listener—and I try to meet each encounter with intention.

When they arrive, the messages are direct. No drama, no small talk. We meet for a reason, and we honor that.

The phrase "Morning Crossovers" started casually and stuck. It became the way I opened the space: "Okay, let's do some Morning Crossovers."

Each message in this book is followed by a reflection—what I call a mourning reflection. These are personal meditations on what each story stirred in me: memories, questions, truths. They're meant to invite you to do the same—to notice what opens in you as you read.

The dead aren't here to haunt us. They come to support, guide, and protect us. Again and again, they show us how to keep going—especially in our hardest moments.

Their stories showed me all that it means to be alive.

I share them in the hope they do the same for you.

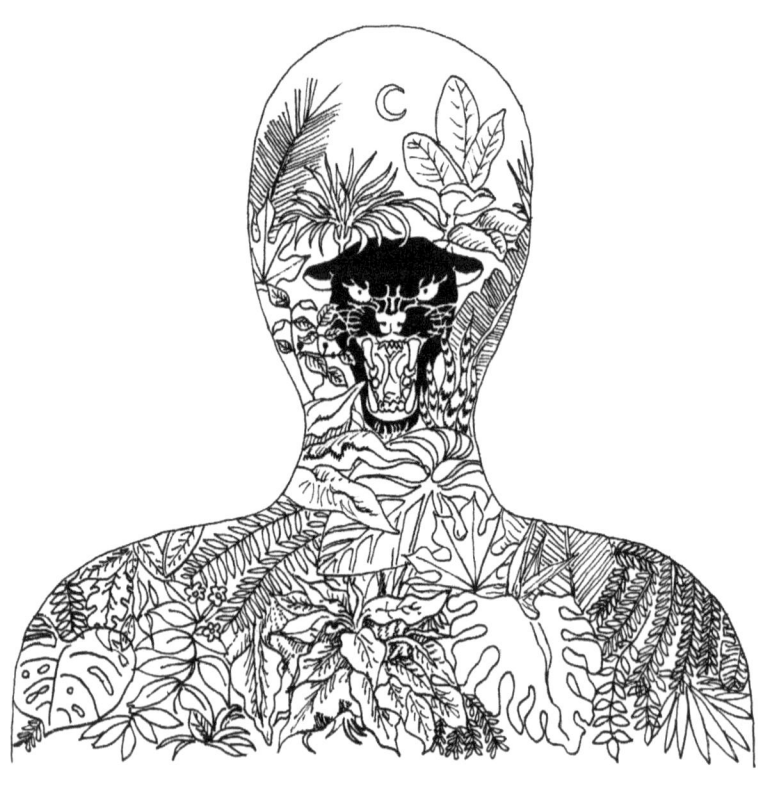

CHAPTER 1

Honey

She said her name was Honey. She was beautiful, soft, and the embodiment of feminine perfection. With luxurious fur draped over her shoulders and wearing a black silk slip dress, her presence was sensual and alluring. She gazed at me quietly with her hazel eyes.

I watched Honey transform from a golden, warm glow into a pale, dark grey with white-filmed eyes. Finger marks gripped purple bruises around her neck. I could see the back of a man's head as he stepped away from her breathless body.

"Husband," she confirmed as he walked out of their house with a hollow ease.

A little black cat appeared and curled up beside her.

I listened and observed, waiting for more.

Suddenly, something started to emerge from another source—not from her or me. With my eyes still closed, I was transported to a different time and place.

A black, shining coat of fur glided gracefully through the brush of rainforest foliage, revealing perfectly sculpted muscles. Golden eyes flashed with obsidian pupils glaring into me—an open-mouthed growl and ivory fangs.

I saw the words "next life."

It was a panther—an apex predator, rare and elusive. Free, feared, and "protected by the gods," this source told me.

I described what I saw to Honey as it moved across my line of sight. She smiled with contentment, thanked me, and then vanished.

After she left, I lay there processing everything I had witnessed. Reflecting on the encounter, I felt honored to have been entrusted with her truth, and despite the context of her circumstances, I remained clear and steady. It felt completely natural and effortless.

Numerous questions raced through my mind, but one thing became clear: I'm meant to do this.

Mourning Reflections

RECLAIMING POWER

Honey's death unfolded tragically in a time and place where her murder went unnoticed, as if she didn't matter—at a time when women were seen as property. Neighbors may have whispered about the incident, but their indifference and the normalization of violence spoke volumes. There were no headlines, no police investigations, and no cries for justice—only her body left behind, which someone would eventually remove and bury.

I understand Honey's next life suggestion: to become something that could tear a man apart and consume him, releasing all that stifled fear and rage.

In the animal kingdom—a realm untouched by our concepts of good and evil—survival is simple, instinctive, and clean. There's no pretense or posturing. Just the raw will to live. And somehow, that feels far less cruel than the things humans do to one another.

I used to believe that reincarnation followed a straight path: starting as amoebas, graduating to plants, then to animals, and finally to humans—the pinnacle of it all. However, I've learned that's not the case.

Sometimes, being human is so painful and violent that a soul might take a long break from this form entirely. We might return as animals—not because it's a step backward, but because it offers relief from human brutality.

In many ways, we are less evolved than animals; we are confused about our collective purpose in the world. We haven't lived on this planet longer than many animal species, yet we still consider ourselves superior. We think we're the most evolved, but we're really the most disconnected.

Do you see yourself as more intelligent than species that have existed for millions of years? Or do they simply understand and fulfill their roles on the planet effectively?

We often underestimate and undervalue the power and intelligence of the natural world. The ecological realm is metaphysical and mysterious in ways we can barely grasp. Most of us wouldn't last a day in the wild on our own, yet we act as if we're in charge.

Until I met Honey, I had never imagined the possibility of being reborn as an apex predator seeking vengeance for the injustices done to us. Noted for future reference.

CHAPTER 2

Susan

I see a woman smiling behind the counter of a cozy bakery. Everything is golden and warm—sunlight streaming through the windows, brown paper bags, and the soft dusting of flour on wood. The smell of fresh bread lingers in the air.

People come and go all day, sharing kindness and laughter. In the midst of it all, Susan beams like a pillar of light. The warmth of the place seems to revolve around her.

As evening arrives, the golden tones cool into shadowy greys. The crowd thins. Susan wipes down the counter and prepares to leave. There's peace in her movements—content, unhurried.

Then the door swings open abruptly.

A man bursts in.

Susan looks up, stunned.

He raises his arm in her direction.

Pop! Pop! Pop!

The room explodes with sound. My view jolts, and she's gone.

Suddenly, we're in a hospital.

Susan lies still, her head wrapped in white gauze, a large tube filling her mouth. Her family surrounds her, silent and devastated, tears streaming down their faces.

Beside her bed, I see her—**her soul**—glowing white, slightly translucent, pacing furiously.

"He was insane!" she shouts. "He thought I was someone else!"

I hear the phrase clearly: **mistaken identity.**

The machines breathe for her, but she has already left her body. The family makes the heart-wrenching decision to let her go.

Susan's spirit doesn't easily cross over. She's caught in the injustice of it all. It wasn't her time. Her life had been good—she loved deeply and was deeply loved. She made people feel like they had come home.

Stranded by the senselessness of her death, she turns to me for what comes next.

I watch a gavel drop, and the image of the scales of justice flickers into sight.

Her death becomes fuel for her next incarnation. Her soul, still full of light, carries a fire now—a devotion to fairness and truth.

Heartbreak becomes passion. Injustice becomes justice.

Susan is born into a privileged, protected life. Her parents—both lawyers—raise her with a sharp awareness and unwavering compassion. She studies hard and works even harder, becoming a powerful advocate who fights for those in her community. Each victory heals something invisible.

Still, there's more to her than the courtroom.

At home, she gathers her neighbors around the table. She bakes, hosts, laughs, and feeds others just like she did in that bakery—extending her love. Once again, she becomes a pillar of light to the people around her.

Susan confidently crosses her arms and nods in agreement, then fades from view.

Mourning Reflections

JUSTICE

When I've faced injustice, it was rarely about the facts—it was about how things were perceived. A lie, a distortion, or a misunderstanding can spiral, casting you as someone you're not. True or false, those impressions influence how people treat you. In Susan's case, that misperception cost her her life.

Injustice reshapes lives, leaving invisible, deeply felt scars. It sabotages careers, fractures communities, and robs people of their peace of mind. These wounds rarely close. They linger, quietly eroding the foundations of who we are. Justice, as we know it, is complicated.

In cases of violent loss, one family seeks accountability, while another wrestles with guilt and context. Legal outcomes vary, often leaving both sides unsettled. A conviction doesn't bring peace to the grieving, and it doesn't ease the pain of those left behind.

There are no easy victories. The grief is palpable, the loss unrelenting—even when a case is legally resolved. No verdict brings back the dead.

While I appreciate the idea that the scales may balance across lifetimes, I wanted to know how to heal from injustice in this one.

Seeking understanding, I turned to the Akashic Records, my trusted source of guidance, for insight on how to navigate the weight of the world's unfairness.

Their answer was simple:

"Enjoy your life."

At first, I resisted. How could that be enough? It's the kind of response that makes you shake your head and roll your eyes.

But the more I sat with it, the more it made sense. When you choose joy, you strip injustice of its power over your life. You reclaim your existence. You liberate yourself from the confines of what was unfair.

The freedom of your spirit is a power only you can choose.

This understanding grounds me whenever I feel the trap of injustice closing in on me.

And when I forget, I return to it like a compass:

Enjoy your life.

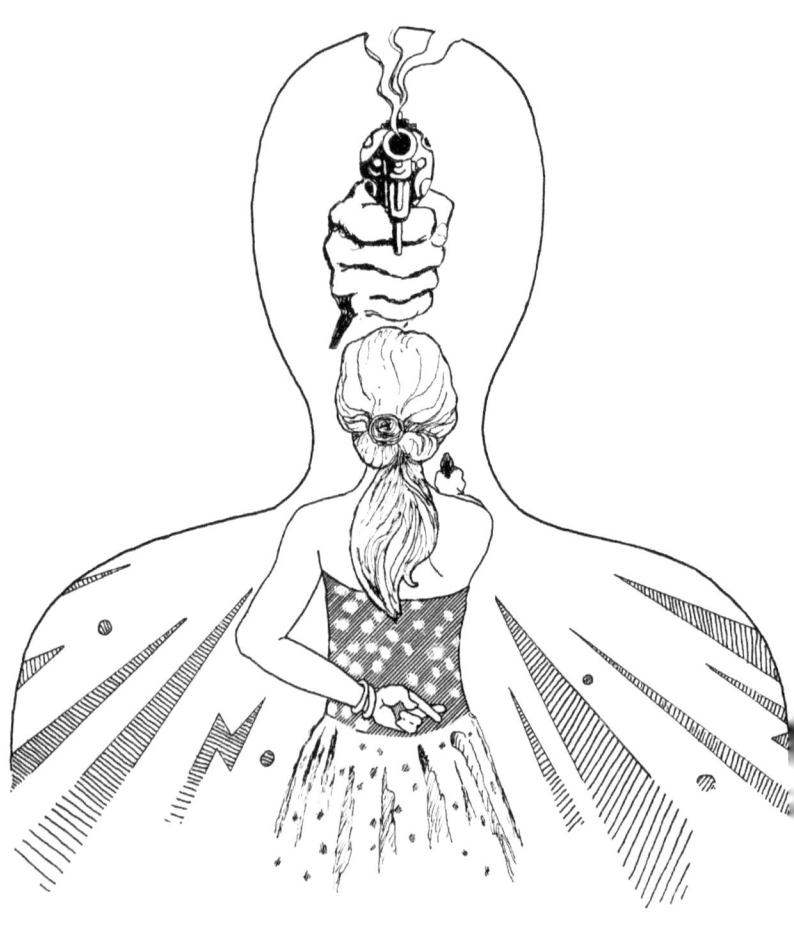

CHAPTER 3

Todd

Todd had always been captivated by beauty—a trait that often clouded his judgment. When he met *her*, he was instantly mesmerized. She had raven-black hair that flowed like a waterfall and green eyes that seemed to pierce through him. Her presence was intoxicating.

He dismissed her jokes about being in the Russian mafia and brushed aside his gut feelings as merely the thrill of her mystery. Choosing fantasy over intuition, he dove headfirst into a whirlwind romance.

Then, one night, she suggested a flirtatious game.

"Close your eyes," she said, teasing. "Let me surprise you."

She blindfolded Todd with a silk scarf. The last thing he saw was her gaze—those hypnotic green eyes—and a small, unsettling smile.

Then, everything shattered.

A sudden gunshot. A flash of pain—and nothing. Darkness swallowed him.

He was gone.

In the space beyond his life, Todd was stunned. She had killed him—not in anger or panic, but with intention. For fun.

Todd couldn't understand how the woman he had loved could end his life as if it meant nothing. Her betrayal was cold and complete. To her, he wasn't even a person—just a plaything in some twisted game. Todd felt foolish, used, and discarded.

"How can I heal from this?" he cried out to me.

I sat quietly, closed my eyes, and listened carefully.

I was shown an image: a fluffy, well-groomed dog, tail wagging, wearing a jeweled collar. A little girl cradles him in her arms, surrounded by a loving family.

Initially, this didn't make sense. It felt too innocent. So, I concentrated more and checked in.

"Yes, keep looking," the Akashic Records confirmed.

Todd is reborn as a cherished family dog in a realm of unconditional love—a purebred companion, adored and protected. Life becomes soft, warm, and filled with affection.

However, the greatest twist is yet to come.

The family that adopts him are descendants of the woman who killed him. Now a grandmother, she is very fond of the dog—of *Todd*—showering him with love every day of his life. The family even treats him better than they treat her.

This next life presents an almost comical poetic balance. Todd receives the unconditional affection he was denied in the past, while she offers him love, unaware of who he once was.

Mourning Reflections

KARMA IS EVERYTHING

When I asked the Akashic Records to clarify the karma in Todd's story, they explained that their karma together revolved around innocence—a stark contrast to their previous life together.

Karma operates in clever and often humorous ways. Rather than a cycle of revenge, it focuses on the wholeness of the soul and presents an alternate version of the story—one that concludes with balance.

It's important to understand that karma isn't about punishment or reward; it's a process of rebalancing. The Akashic Records describe karma as:

"What you create, you will recreate—until you create something new."

How we exit this life carries energetic threads that can intertwine with our future experiences. Our impact stretches far beyond what we can see in a single lifetime.

One conversation, action, and moment of impact can create ripples that extend across generations and multiple lifetimes. We seldom see the entire arc of what we've set in motion.

As karma unfolds, those who have hurt us the most can become our fiercest protectors or greatest loves. The worst betrayals can be redefined through loyalty and lasting companionship. Even the deepest wounds can gradually soften and heal over time.

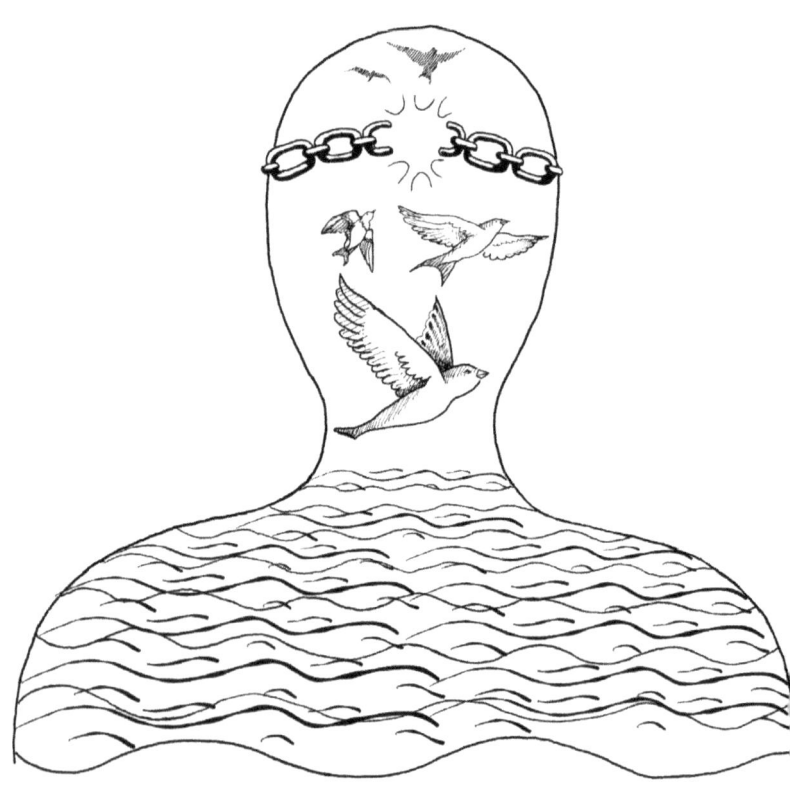

CHAPTER 4

Five Men

I see a man in wet shoes, his pants cinched at the ankles by heavy chains. My eyes follow the chain to another man behind him and then to another. They are linked together in a line, their heads tilted down.

The men are on a boat slick with water, the glossy white fiberglass tinted blue by the night sky and moonlight. They were on their way somewhere hopeful, until they realized they had been deceived and would never arrive.

An unchained man stands beside them and pushes the first one off the back of the boat. One by one, each man is pushed over the edge and sinks. The silence is striking; there are no voices, yelling, or fighting, only the "thunk" of water splashing in succession.

Five men: husbands, fathers, brothers, uncles, sons.

A final whirlpool stops spinning and settles into the rhythm of the waves. The boat speeds away.

Then, I find myself in a kitchen where a family is consumed by panic. They cry and pace back and forth, shouting questions at one another, their voices filled with fear and their hearts heavy with uncertainty.

Concern for their missing loved ones looms over them. Years of anguish and nightmares have left them tormented, and the pain of their loss has never subsided.

For the men, the repercussions of their disappearances deeply affected everyone in their lives, causing them to lose faith in humanity. They no longer want to be human again.

Through their sorrow, the Akashic Records reveal a chain shattering into pieces. The fragments then transform into small yellow birds flying together toward the sun. The Records tell me to encourage them to become birds, to fly freely and lightly, high above the world's heaviness and suffering.

Mourning Reflections

MIGRATION IS FREEDOM

Migration isn't just a right—it's a necessity woven into the fabric of life itself. The instinct to move lives in all of us, a vital part of how we survive, adapt, and respond to the shifting landscapes of our world.

But the path of migration is rarely easy. The story of the five men reveals just how harsh it can be—how fear, scarcity, and greed can close doors and turn people into threats. It's a reminder of how quickly the ground beneath us can shift, how what feels stable one day can unravel the next.

In my search for understanding amidst the world's current chaos—climate change, civil unrest, displacement—I turned to the Akashic Records for insight. Their message was clear: **Migration is only going to become more common. But they didn't say it with fear. They said it with hope and a gentle instruction: "Let's move around nicely."**

That has stayed with me. Because it's not just about the movement—it's about how we treat each other in the process. How we show up when people are forced to leave everything behind. How we open our hearts and our homes, even when it's uncomfortable.

Our survival depends on that kindness. On remembering that any one of us could be in that position, just one unexpected moment away from needing refuge ourselves. Safety and privilege can slip away faster than we think.

We live in a divided world. The gaps feel wide and are getting wider. And still—what will it take for us to see one another clearly again? To remember our shared humanity?

Change starts inside. In our thoughts, our choices, our willingness to shift. We can't afford to wait.

CHAPTER 5

Ellen

She tells me her name is Ellen, but after the accident, she began calling herself "Hell-en." Her life had become a living hell.

"It was like I had two names, two faces," she explains. "A split personality. After the car crash, one part of me died, and the other stayed behind. I was paralyzed—trapped inside a body that wouldn't move. I could feel everything but couldn't respond. I was screaming on the inside. I hated myself. I fell apart. And over time, it wore my spirit down. I eventually died from heart complications. I was heartbroken—literally—watching myself waste away, bursting from the inside. The pain of being stuck in that contorted, lifeless body was unbearable."

In her next life, Ellen returns as a dancer.

Free from paralysis, she moves with grace—fluid, radiant, alive. She glides across stages around the world, each dance a prayer of freedom, each step a celebration of being. Audiences watch, spellbound. She becomes a symbol of vitality and liberation, proof that movement can be medicine, and beauty a kind of truth.

But Ellen doesn't dance only for herself.

She carries a deep compassion for others who feel trapped—in their bodies, their grief, their silence. She knows that kind of pain intimately. And she knows that real freedom isn't just about what we overcome—it's also about what we offer.

So she teaches.

She guides others to move beyond limitation, to reconnect with the parts of themselves that ache to be seen, felt, and freed. In her presence, others feel something shift. As if her dancing awakens something long asleep inside them—a flicker of movement, a breath of possibility.

Ellen's journey shows us that the body can be both a prison and a passageway. That through it, we can remember who we really are.

Mourning Reflections

THE EMBODIED SPIRIT

At its heart, Ellen's story is a powerful reckoning with the body—how we live in it, leave it, resent it, and ultimately return to it. Her experience reveals the tension between the urge to escape our physical limitations and the deeper human need to connect with our embodied selves.

In times of pain, trauma, or illness, it's natural to dissociate—to float above the discomfort or numb ourselves entirely. But when we abandon our bodies, we often abandon part of our soul's purpose, too. Ellen shows us that even when the body becomes a place of unbearable suffering, our spirit is still moving. Still becoming.

One client I worked with described her chronic depression as feeling like she was carrying the weight of the entire Earth. Every step felt heavy, impossible. During her Akashic Records session, we discovered that in a previous lifetime she had been a light, ethereal being—playful, floating, nearly weightless. She had chosen to incarnate on Earth to learn grounding. But she hadn't expected gravity—the literal and emotional kind—to feel so overwhelming.

When this truth came through, she laughed. It wasn't that her burden disappeared overnight, but her relationship with it shifted. She began to see her struggle more externally. And that changed everything.

Our bodies tell stories through posture, pain, and movement. They carry memory—both personal and ancestral. And while we're often taught to fix or fight them, Ellen's story offers another way: to soften into them. To listen. To honor their limitations without confusing them with the limits of our spirit.

Ellen didn't just escape her paralysis—she alchemized it. In her next life, she dances not just for herself, but for those still trapped in their own bodies. She becomes a living invitation: to move, to feel, to become free.

Like Ellen, we don't need perfect bodies to live with grace.

We need presence.

And a willingness to return to the body as a sacred companion— flawed, miraculous, and always full of possibility.

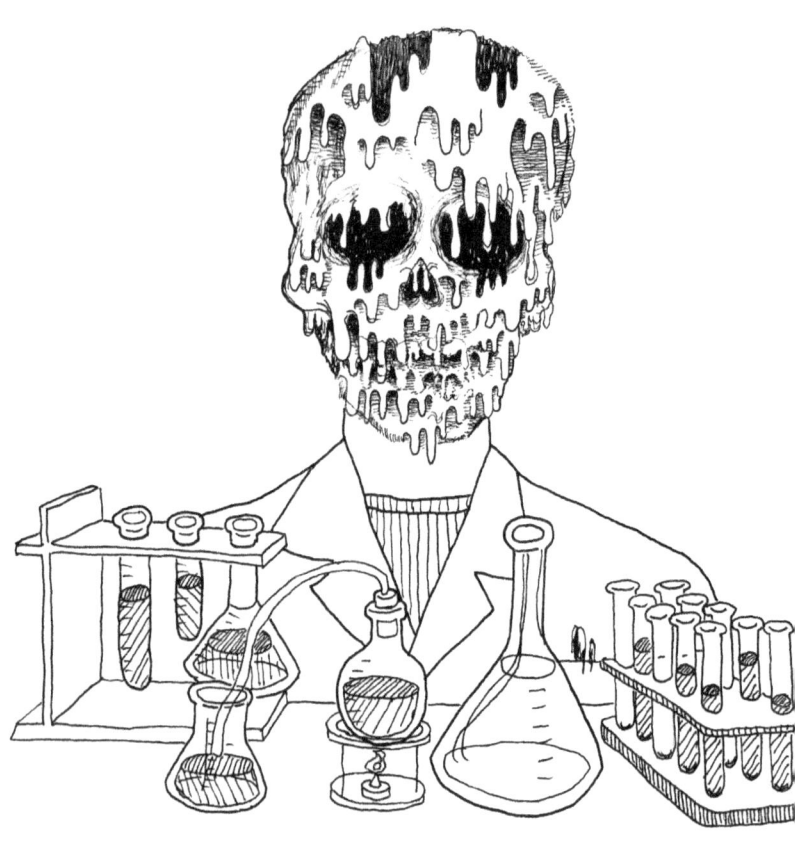

CHAPTER 6

Stephanie

A woman introduces herself as Stephanie. She explains that she was a scientist—a chemist specifically.

"A chemical reaction exploded in my face. I felt every second of it. It was unbearable—the torture. My whole face melted to the bone in an instant. Then came the stillness. The suffering. It was a lethal weapon: chemical warfare."

She pauses, then continues.

"I was silenced for knowing the truth. The secret was considered more important than my life. I was terrified. But they were afraid of me, too. I couldn't win.

I survived the incident, but I lived shattered. The testing had gone wrong, and I knew it. I just wanted the torment to end.

In the end, they killed me for it. They were relentless.

I needed to escape—my body, the threat, the fear, the misery. All of it.

I welcomed death.

What they did was evil. The men of science saw me as expendable because I was a woman. So many women have suffered in the name of science—whether working in the field or being used in it.

Men are terrifying. I hold so much pain from that lifetime.

I don't know how to return.

I don't know how to feel safe."

In the Akashic Records, a vision unfolds. I see a rural community in the woods—rooted in deep Indigenous tradition, but it lies in the future.

I hear the words: **"Woman is sacred."**

A matriarchal community leads, guided by a grandmother and her lineage of women. Life there moves with nature: slow, steady, harmonious. Plant medicines line the shelves. Laughter rings through the trees. Their days are soft, joyful, and free.

They live far from the mainstream—away from the systems of science, medicine, and society that once harmed them.

Here, the men are kind. Caring. Strong. Honest. They listen. They do the work. They protect and honor the women. No one is diminished.

It's a modern, visionary Indigenous community—one that lives with integrity, health, and freedom.

Stephanie is safe there. Valued. Uplifted. Her knowledge is honored. Her life is protected.

Mourning Reflection

THE COST OF KNOWING

Some truths carry a high cost. Stephanie's story is one of them.

She wasn't just hurt in a lab accident—she was betrayed. Silenced for what she knew, discarded because she was a woman, and seen as a threat instead of a person. That kind of pain doesn't fade easily. It stays in the nervous system, in the memory of what it meant to be unsafe, unprotected, and alone.

There's a long pattern here. Women in science—brilliant women, curious women, intuitive women—have been treated as disposable. Used, tested, dismissed. Sometimes it's subtle. Sometimes, like with Stephanie, it's deadly.

And still, she knew something real. Something that mattered.

It's easy to romanticize knowledge, to talk about truth like it always sets us free. But for many people—especially those pushed to the margins—knowing the truth can be dangerous. It can make you a target. It can cost you everything.

Even so, truth finds a way.

In the Records, I saw a different future. One where knowledge is protected by community. One where safety isn't an exception, but a given. Where people know how to care for each other, not just in theory, but in practice.

That vision isn't an escape from reality. It's a reminder that something better is possible.

Stephanie's story is a warning, but it's also a call to remember. To pay attention. To stop discarding the people who carry uncomfortable truths. And to build a world where no one has to choose between silence and survival.

CHAPTER 7

Marcus

He tells me his name is Marcus.

"Old age, young heart," he says. "I wasn't ready to go. I wasn't done yet. I had to let go of my dreams. I felt cut off. There was more inside me—I wanted to begin again. Please help me do that."

The words, **"boy genius"** surface in the Records.

The Akashic field surrounds him with love and encouragement. He's invited to return as a child prodigy—one whose brilliance and creativity flow freely from the heart. This time, he'll pick up where he left off, with all of his gifts intact.

"Young age, old soul," the Records whisper.

In this new life, Marcus shines. His intelligence and natural talent come through early, allowing him to do what once felt out of reach. The dreams that had to be set down now have space to bloom.

Mourning Reflections

UNFINISHED BUSINESS

Marcus reminds me: The soul never gives up on its dreams.

His story invites me to reflect on genius—how it sometimes reappears early in life, like a continuation of something unfinished.

Some children are not just gifted—they're remembering.

The prodigy who picks up a violin and plays with ancient precision… The poet who writes like they've seen too much for their age… Maybe they're not just smart. Maybe they've been here before.

Marcus reminds me that souls return not just to heal, but to complete what once felt impossible. Genius might not be rare—it might just be recycled brilliance.

I remember a boy in middle school who was already taking college courses. He wore sweaters like an old professor and spoke like one, too. Was he, like Marcus, returning to finish what had once been interrupted?

Life isn't linear. It spirals. Every life builds on the last. Every loss, lesson, and love adds to the tapestry. Death doesn't end the story—it returns you to your essence.

You enter each lifetime carrying the wisdom and longings of the ones before. That continuity is hope. That persistence is power.

Remember:

You are lifetimes strong.Lifetimes capable.

Lifetimes becoming.

And yes, that's also why you may feel lifetimes exhausted.

You're not starting from scratch. You're continuing a masterpiece.

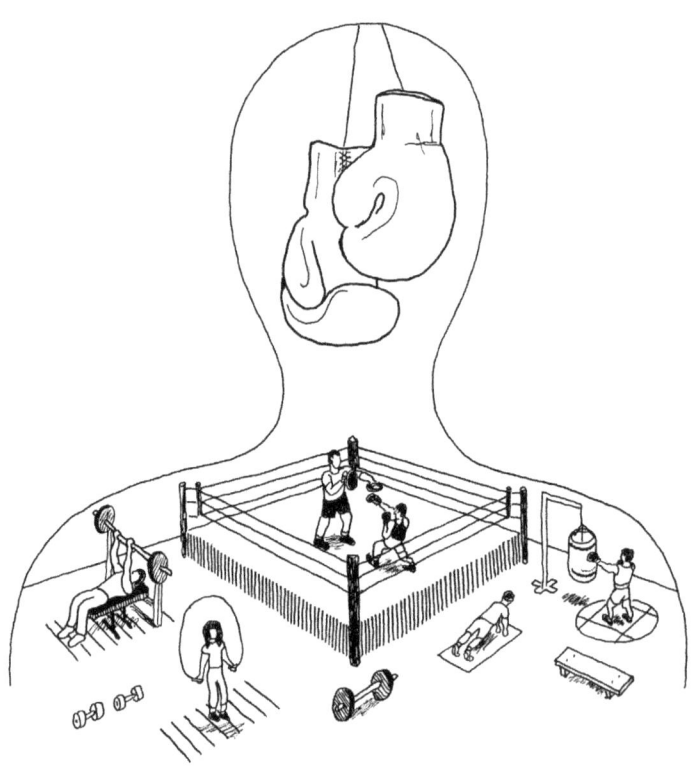

CHAPTER 8

Elizabeth

Elizabeth approaches reincarnation with a cautious heart. There's a fear that's kept her from wanting to return.

She tells me, "I was stalked and murdered in cold blood while walking home alone one night. I'm afraid of predators—they're still everywhere, hiding in plain sight. From here, in Spirit, I can keep a closer watch on them. But when you're alive, it's harder. They mask themselves well. I don't know who I'd be or how. I want to be a woman again. I miss it. I miss feeling free. But I don't think I'd be safe. Not now. Not with the world the way it is."

I nod and close my eyes, asking to see what's possible for her next life.

A vision comes: a group of rowdy boys in a living room, laughing and wrestling. Just outside their chaos stands a beautiful teenage girl, smiling and giggling. One of the boys scoops her up and carries her into the huddle—this girl is Elizabeth.

This time, she's born into a family of fighters. Tough boys. Strong men. A father who raises them all alone after losing his wife too soon. Her brothers are wild and protective. Her father is steady and full of love.

In this life, Elizabeth is surrounded by strength. Her family teaches her what real protection looks like—how to hold her ground with presence, how to set boundaries without apology, how to trust what she feels. She grows into someone powerful and confident.

Her mother, though gone, never really leaves. She stays close as a guide, whispering wisdom from beyond. Elizabeth learns to see beneath the surface of people and situations, like she's always reading between the lines. She can spot danger without fear. She knows when to walk away and when to stand her ground.

Boxing becomes her craft and her medicine. She teaches kids how to fight—but more than that, how to feel strong and alive in their own skin. How to move through the world with clarity, joy, and connection.

The trauma of her past becomes fuel. She rises, not just for herself, but for every child who's ever felt afraid. In the ring and in life, Elizabeth becomes a force—one who transforms fear into power and pain into purpose. With every punch, every lesson, every laugh shared with her students, she helps build a world where it's safe to be soft and strong. Safe to be free.

Mourning Reflection

I love how, in her next life, Elizabeth finds a supportive family—a loving group of men who protect her and give her a foundation of safety and strength. It reminds me how transformative a nurturing environment can be. When we feel protected, we can begin to grow into who we really are.

Even with support, vulnerability remains. Many of us can relate to Elizabeth's fear and understand how quickly an ordinary moment can turn threatening. Her story makes me grateful for the intuitive sense that lets me know when something feels off. It brings to mind the close calls I've had—and how I've learned to listen to that quiet inner voice, even when it doesn't make logical sense.

Like Elizabeth, I live in the tension between wanting to live fully and needing to feel safe. That push and pull runs deep. There are times I want to leap into something new, but I hold back—not from fear exactly, but from awareness. Caution has become part of how I move. A second skin.

It's not always comfortable, but it's real. And it's taught me that vigilance doesn't have to close us off—it can deepen our relationship to ourselves, to others, and to life. Our intuition is a gift, not just for survival, but for clarity. It shows us what's true, even when nothing is said out loud.

Support and self-awareness go hand in hand. One helps create the conditions for the other. Elizabeth becomes a protector because she is protected. She finds strength not because the world is suddenly safe, but because she understands how unsafe it can be—and chooses to live fully anyway.

That, to me, is real empowerment. It's not pretending we're fearless. It's choosing to show up with our eyes open, with our hearts intact. To teach, to love, to create, to guide—even when we know the risks.

CHAPTER 9

Frederick

One afternoon, while sitting on my living room couch, I felt a familiar prompt—one of my deceased friends wanted to connect. To my surprise, it was my first killer.

Curious, I closed my eyes and focused. The first image that came to mind was the face of actor James Gandolfini—not as himself, but as a reference to *The Sopranos*. This energy felt heavy.

He introduced himself as Frederick, but insisted I call him Freddie.

"I used to be a mob boss," he said. "A bad guy. Not the cool kind—the evil kind. I was violent, paranoid, and cruel. I caused so much suffering, and I feel terrible about it. I want to come back and do good this time. I want to make it right. I'm not looking to relive that life or the pain I caused. I just genuinely want to do better. I want to atone."

This time, the Akashic Records opened with context. They aimed to uncover the root of Freddie's past-life behavior, then offered insight into his potential next incarnation.

Here's what the Records shared:

"Seeds are sown for morals and values. Trust your instincts. In your new life, you'll live differently. You weren't born evil—you reacted out of fear. You feared death and being hunted. Your beliefs created a world ruled by fear. You approached life through the lens of survival, always accumulating more fear and lashing out in response.

In your next life, that fear will ease. If you feel scared, it will come from within—not from outside threats. You'll be safe. Your karma is subtle but persistent. Early life may feel anxious, but as you move through it, you'll discover peace.

Letting go of old beliefs will be hard in childhood, but by your teen years, you'll develop balance and inner sturdiness. Trust your heart to lead you away from fear. Courage will rise from your vulnerability.

Your parents will reflect your soul's work: Your mother—a bit neurotic and triggering—will help you release karma. Your father—headstrong and grounded—will stabilize you. Seek a couple with these dynamics in a place near where you once lived. You can return to the same town if you like. Revisiting that place will help repair what you once damaged.

In this new life, you'll still feel reactive at times. You may have the urge to harm or lash out—echoes from your past. Stay alert. These temptations will be subtle, but they are yours to outgrow."

Freddie accepted the message and seemed comforted. Still, I couldn't shake the concern that a violent tendency might linger beneath the surface. Before we closed our connection, I made sure to emphasize the importance of vigilance.

Mourning Reflection

REDEMPTION AND THE DARKNESS WITHIN

The Akashic Records offer an outlook free of judgment, allowing us to see everything and everyone from the highest perspective. They recognize the balance of light and dark within us and offer guidance through that lens.

We've all lived countless lives—kings, queens, slaves, animals. At some point, we've been each other. In that light, judgment becomes meaningless. Our shared experience across lifetimes gives rise to compassion.

Like Freddie's story, our earliest challenges can shape us into more empathetic and grounded adults. However, that isn't always the case. Trauma more often perpetuates cycles of violence, fear, or emotional shutdown. Pain doesn't automatically make us wise—it depends on how it's met, supported, and processed.

While outcomes vary, adversity can spark a desire to create something better for others—but only when we feel safe enough to reflect and choose a different path.

Think about your own life: What difficult moments helped shape you? What valuable lessons or unexpected gifts came from those times?

Freddie's journey reminds us how important it is to find healthy ways to move through intense emotions. Our darker feelings carry meaning. Anger, for example, can shield us from grief. Aggression

71

might mask fear. These defenses are part of being human. When we ignore them, they can become heavy and harmful—to ourselves or others.

The darkness within us is rich with insight and intensity. It holds passion, intuition, and a drive for transformation. It deserves a safe space to be acknowledged and expressed.

When we make peace with our shadow, we begin to come home to ourselves. Redemption becomes possible—not through perfection, but through the courage to hold both our light and our dark.

Our shadow doesn't make us broken; it makes us whole. When we welcome it with compassion, we access a deeper kind of power—rooted, embodied, magnetic. It draws others in not because it hides the dark, but because it honors it. Wholeness is what makes us real. And in that wholeness, we become our full and true selves.

CHAPTER 10

Evelyn

"I was walking home one night when someone attacked me from the dark woods near my house. I was so close to getting inside, just a few feet from my door, when he grabbed me. He smashed my head with a stone. It cracked my skull. I bled out. I felt the blood leak from my brain into the ground, soaking into the Earth.

I couldn't get up. I was in shock, disconnected from my body. He hit me with such force, I went limp. I felt trapped—so close to home and safety, but unable to reach it. I faded in and out of consciousness, lying on the ground, staring at the warm light inside my house. It was waiting for me, but I couldn't get to it.

I held on as long as I could, trying to move my fingers, hands, and legs. My body gave out, but my mind stayed alert. Everything slowed down. All I could do was beg for mercy, for release from angels, from God. I pleaded to be set free from the pain, from my body. Death felt like the only relief. The fear was unbearable—fear of being trapped, and fear of what came next.

I watched that window of light until I couldn't anymore. I let go and surrendered to silence.

I don't know how to return. When? Where? With whom? I want to come back. But I don't know how to do it safely.

Can you see something good for me? A place? A person to be? I need safety. I need to move freely."

I saw a newborn baby, cradled in loving hands.

Evelyn is born into a nurturing community—a village rooted in care. She grows up surrounded by women who embody warmth and wisdom: doulas, midwives, mothers. Together, they form a sisterhood dedicated to the well-being of every child. Their love is a kind of shelter, soft and strong.

In this world, Evelyn thrives. Protective "mama bears" watch over her fiercely. Men offer their presence and strength, but it's the women who lead. It's a matriarchal circle where everyone is seen, held, and valued.

As Evelyn grows, she finds her place in this vibrant web of connection. The community's shared devotion to care shapes her life and ripples outward, becoming a legacy of tenderness that endures.

Mourning Reflections

PEOPLE ARE THE SHELTER

There's a deep desire in all of us to feel safe and at home in the world, surrounded by people who love and support us. That longing shaped Evelyn's story. In her final moments, she lay just feet from her house, watching the warm light through the windows, unable to reach it. The nearness of safety—and the heartbreak of being locked out—stayed with me.

In her next life, everything shifts—this time, the light finds her. She is born into loving arms, surrounded by tenderness. She is welcomed home the moment she arrives. The light she couldn't reach before is now the very first thing she sees. It doesn't erase what happened, but it completes what was left unfinished. That threshold between life and death becomes the beginning of her healing.

When a baby is born, joy rises. People gather. Tears fall. In that tenderness something shifts—we remember what matters. We glimpse a better future, and with it comes a quiet vow: to love more fiercely, to protect what's fragile.

Our relationships—families, communities, chosen kin—become our shelter. They carry us through what the world cannot prevent. We lean on one another, lifting each other up, creating spaces where safety is not just a hope but a practice.

Evelyn's story reminds us how quickly life can change, how vulnerable we all are, and how vital it is to strengthen the bonds that hold us—not just in moments of crisis but always.

The places we cherish may become sources of sorrow. But it's the people who fill those places with care who make them home—the ones who stay, who show up, who love.

Even in loss, the presence of good people becomes a kind of home. A reminder that we are not alone. And that healing can begin the moment someone chooses to welcome us in.

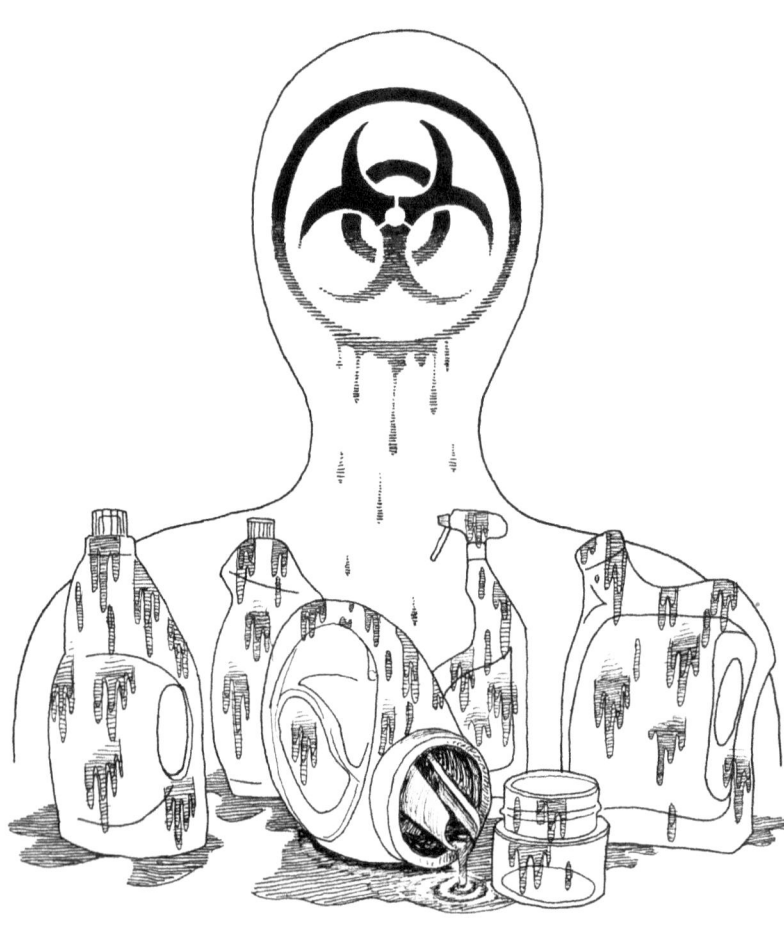

CHAPTER 11

Alison

A woman named Alison reached out to share her story.

She explained that she had been peacefully asleep when a wave of nausea washed over her. Jolted awake, she felt disoriented and unwell, confused by the sudden onset of illness. As she tried to piece together what had happened, a startling realization came: She had been poisoned.

Alison was a devoted mother of two young boys. On that tragic day, her children—innocently curious—had mixed household cleaners into her drink. They had recently learned about poisons in school and, not fully understanding the dangers, didn't believe anything bad could actually happen.

The vibrant rhythm of their family life was shattered. Alison died, leaving her sons to bear the weight of a heartbreaking mistake. The incident sent shockwaves through the community and prompted changes in how schools approached safety education around toxins in the home.

Even in Spirit, Alison's primary concern was her sons. She knew they would carry the weight of guilt, sorrow, and confusion for the rest of their lives, and she wanted to know how—if—they would heal.

In their next lives, Alison's sons would be highly sensitive to toxins, reacting strongly to substances commonly found in everyday products. This hypersensitivity would draw them toward the outdoors, where the air is clean and nature feels like medicine.

They would be reborn as siblings or meet again as close friends, transforming past guilt into purposeful action. Together, they would dedicate themselves to creating gentle, non-toxic home goods—natural cleaners, environmentally friendly materials, and safer everyday products.

With that comfort, the reading shifted to a glimpse of Alison's next life.

She returns as a nutritionist focused on gut health, deeply influenced by the poisoning of her past. Believing that food is medicine, she specializes in natural, holistic nutrition. In this new chapter, she chooses not to have children but finds joy in her pets—two fluffy dogs and a talkative parrot.

She lives with her husband, a psychologist. Together, they explore the connection between nutrition and mental health, discovering intuitive overlaps in their work.

The Akashic Records reveal a unique insight Alison uncovers: a strong link between fruit and intuition. She and her husband travel to share their research, helping others detoxify their bodies while exploring the relationship between instinct, the mind, and food.

Although Alison and her sons never meet again in this lifetime, their work holds deep resonance. While her sons focus on purifying the physical environment, Alison turns her attention inward—

clearing and nourishing the internal home: the body. Together, across lifetimes, they remain united in their devotion to healing.

Mourning Reflections

HEALING THROUGH PURPOSE

We don't always remember where our pain began—but we can still feel its influence.

Alison's sons will likely never remember their past lives or how that tragedy shaped them. For most people, exploring past lives isn't part of their personal growth or self-understanding. Yet their instinct to create safer environments, their sensitivity to toxins, and their desire to protect are not random. These impulses are the soul's way of healing through purpose.

That sense of purpose doesn't come from nowhere—it often grows out of old pain, even if we don't remember the source.

Healing isn't just about recovering from what hurt us. It's about turning pain into something meaningful. When we channel it into what we care about, it becomes direction—it becomes service.

Sometimes that drive shows up as a deep sense of responsibility or a strong urge to change something. We may not know why it matters so much to us, but that feeling is often a clue.

The people closest to us—our friends, family, partners, and colleagues—can help us see these patterns more clearly. They act as mirrors, reflecting what we believe, what we fear, and where we're being asked to grow. Through reflection, therapy, or spiritual practices, we start to see how the past (known or unknown) shapes what we're here to do now.

You don't need to remember a past life to heal from one. Just pay attention to what keeps coming up—what bothers you, what calls to you, and where you keep getting stuck. Those patterns point to what's asking for healing.

For Alison's sons, healing looks like creating safer homes. For Alison, it's about helping others rebuild their health. Even though they never cross paths again, they stay connected through the work they do—each offering their form of care and restoration.

So ask yourself:

What does healing look like for me now?

You may not remember the original wound, but your choices, values, and passions already know the way forward.

CHAPTER 12

Jonathon

Jonathon was stabbed through the heart—from both sides at once—a moment that echoed not just through him but through his enemies as well. The scene zoomed out, revealing a vast panorama of battlefields strewn with soldiers crumbling all around.

In that instant, he saw it—the regret and rejection of their mission—in the eyes of the man standing before him, mirrored in the fearful gaze of the soldier behind. None of them wanted to be there. None wanted to carry out these actions.

Trying to mediate the chaos, Jonathon found himself caught in the attack, fully absorbing its immediate impact—and the end of his own life.

As Jonathon recounted his death, the Records revealed an image: a peacock collapsed on the ground, its once-vibrant feathers dulling to gray. The vision flickered—like a glitch—between the peacock and a soldier's lifeless body.

"I felt so sorry for them," he said. "I died trying to mediate the situation. I sacrificed myself."

The fading peacock wasn't just a symbol—it was them. Once radiant, now broken. Their colors drained by the weight of regret.

The Akashic Records responded, steady and clear: **"You died with truth and integrity."** This message marked the turning point—his next transformation.

In his new chapter, Jonathon becomes a heart-centered champion—a defender of love within organizations that honor heart-focused values. The trauma of his past fuels a profound compassion for the world.

I see him smiling, dressed in an army vest and bandana, straight out of the 1970s. Images of anti-war protests, the Woodstock dove, and peace parades blend with a hint of futuristic vision.

At his core, Jonathon still carries the soul of a soldier—powerful, courageous, yet endearing and magnetic. He embodies the healthy, future divine masculine: a big, open heart guiding his strength. His wisdom about war and violence stems from his lived experience, even though he no longer faces those battles in this lifetime.

When he speaks of love and battlefields, he breaks down barriers, melting hearts and inspiring those around him to open theirs. His presence alone transforms and uplifts everyone he meets.

The Records reveal Jonathon as an initiator of peaceful movements—led by compassionate authorities forming groups dedicated to positive change in their communities. He inspires transformation in once-feared leaders, contributing to the rise of a powerful movement.

With a grin and a wink, Jonathon flashes me a peace sign before slowly fading away.

Mourning Reflection

THE PEACEFUL WARRIOR

In the past life readings I've done, death in battle shows up a lot. It's especially common for people with heart or lung issues in this life—many of them went through trauma in those areas before, often being shot or stabbed in the chest. At this point, I'd say almost everyone has lived through war in one form or another.

World War II and the Holocaust come up often. And there's usually a split in how those souls respond to reincarnation. Some endured such immense suffering that they have chosen to avoid human existence altogether. Others returned right away, determined to prevent that kind of devastation from happening again. You might be one of those people.

It's worth noticing how you feel about certain wars in history. Is there one you've always felt strongly about? Do certain images or memories show up that don't seem to come from your current life?

Warfare runs deep in the collective. Even as we've changed, it still shows up again and again—about once every century. I asked the Akashic Records why we keep repeating the same patterns, and they said, **"There's a collective belief that history repeats itself— but it doesn't have to. You have countless other choices to make."**

They're right. As a society, we still resort to force when things become difficult. When conflict escalates, we default to destruction. It's uncommon for us to slow down enough to consider other approaches—diplomacy, collaboration, creative problem-solving.

We're conditioned to fight. But what actually results from that? Do the issues get resolved? Not really. Or not in a way that addresses the depth of the damage that's been inflicted.

If we're serious about evolving, we have to look at how we respond to conflict. There are other ways forward, but they take intention—and practice.

That's why Jonathon's story resonates with me. People like him remind me of what's possible. I think about him often and hope he's already returned to do the important work of building something better. His energy is strong and steady, and it makes me believe we're not stuck. We have the power to choose differently.

Because no one really wins a war. Even when someone claims victory, the damage lingers—sometimes for generations. That impact isn't always visible, but it doesn't go away.

Each of us has a role in shifting that cycle. Peace doesn't show up on its own—we have to participate in it.

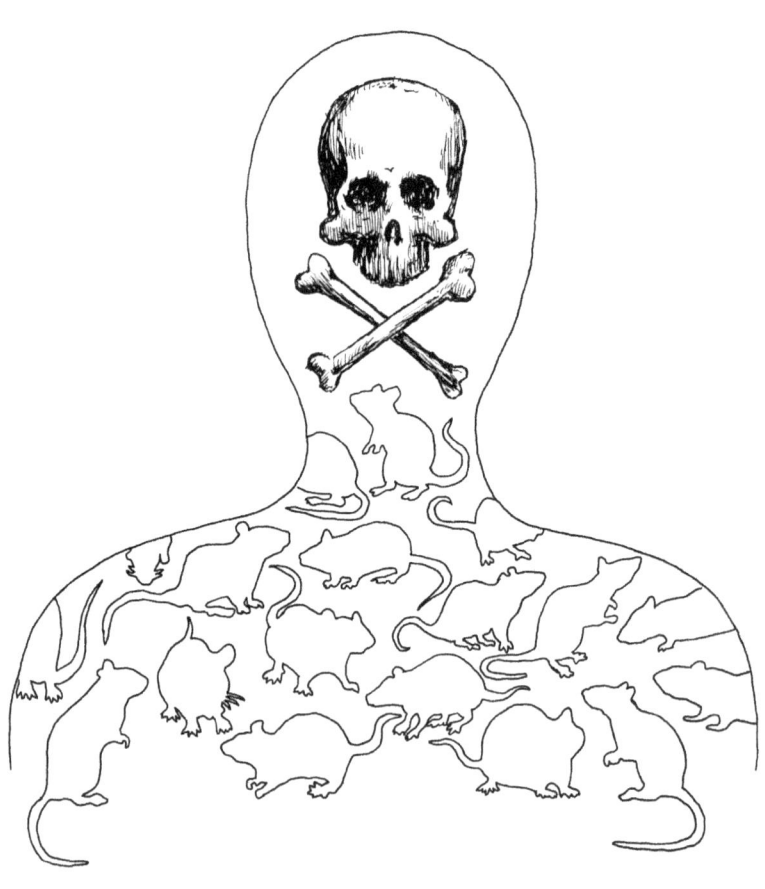

CHAPTER 13

Ethan

Ethan introduces himself.

I see dead skin—stretched thin over a lifeless body. The image is stark, unflinching.

"Rotten. Sick. Left for dead. Neglected," Ethan says.

"There was a sickness in the air," he continues. "The plague. A time when the sick were treated like zombies—feared, abandoned. They suffered without even a broth to comfort them."

He looked so ill that he resembled a living corpse—alone and uncared for.

"Being sick made you a pariah," he continues. "People were terrified of catching it. The sick were abandoned when they needed care the most. It was a rotten world. Sickness infected everything—bodies, minds, even the fear itself.

To be alive but look dead was unimaginable. I died of starvation because I couldn't feed myself. No doctors came. No caregivers. A woman was assigned to care for me, but she caught the plague too. There was nothing anyone could do."

He shows me rats feeding on the dead, tearing through rotting flesh. "The rats are evil," he says. "It was the darkest of times."

I see a balloon float upwards—a wish for better days.

Then the scene shifts. I'm shown glimpses of Ethan's potential future life.

A boy runs up a sunlit hill, dressed in overalls and a button-up shirt.

"As a young man, he is a gardener who cultivates connection and healing through rich plants and medicine," the Akashic Records share.

I describe the vision to Ethan:

"You're born into a culture that reveres the healing properties of plants. Your instinct for medicine is rooted in the soil. Your family treats illness with ancient remedies drawn from the natural world.

As you grow, you become self-sufficient. Your shelves fill with tinctures, herbs, and spices. You're raised in a community that values care and healing. When disaster comes, you're resourceful—and generous.

You pursue a formal medical education, but your path stretches beyond hospital walls. You merge traditional healing with scientific insight to serve others.

Your studies take you across cultures, exploring diverse plants and their uses. You gain a deep understanding of both natural and man-made illnesses and the medicines that can address them.

You are trusted, beloved. A doctor of the future, rooted in ancient tradition."

Ethan smiles. "Good for it!" he says brightly, then adds, "Where?"

The Records reveal a map. The Netherlands is highlighted.

"This community is deeply interconnected and nurturing," they explain. **"It allows you to focus and become who you are meant to be."**

Mourning Reflection

DEATH BY ISOLATION

Ethan's death wasn't solely due to the plague, but also to the absence of human connection. While the setting may seem distant, the feelings are not. We understand what it's like to be isolated, afraid, to witness systems failing the most vulnerable.

During the COVID-19 pandemic, we saw how quickly fear could unravel our connections. People died alone. Families were kept apart. The emotional toll—grief, addiction, depression—was just as real as the physical one. Isolation doesn't just break the body. It breaks the spirit. It drains the will to live.

Years later, we're still grappling with the mental and emotional aftershocks. The pandemic's effects remain poignant, even as we try to move forward. And still, the most vulnerable continue to suffer.

But through the shift in Ethan's story, we glimpse something else—a life rooted in belonging. A life held by community, guided by purpose, and nourished by the natural world. His return to connection—both human and earthly—shows us that while isolation wounds, connection heals.

We aren't meant to navigate life—or illness—alone. The presence of others can pull us back from the edge. Sometimes, it only takes one person, one act of care, to change a fate.

Ethan's story reminds us of both the cost of disconnection and the promise of what's possible when we choose to show up for one another.

Connection is survival. And every time we reach out, every time we care, we choose life over fear.

CHAPTER 14

Spirits Across State Lines

Most of my spiritual connections have happened in the Hudson Valley area of New York, where I'm from. But I began to wonder: What would it be like to connect with the dead in places unfamiliar to me? Curious, I planned a solo road trip from New York to Savannah, Georgia.

Part of my inspiration came from a friend who'd stayed at the famously haunted Marshall House in Savannah. When she returned, she was full of ghost stories—so vivid and specific they mirrored my own early experiences with mediumship. Her symptoms, sensations, even her language… I recognized it all. I told her she was a medium. She didn't resist the idea. In fact, she embraced it—and then insisted I visit the hotel myself.

At the time, I felt brave enough to venture into a place known for ghostly encounters. I thought I could handle it. I seriously underestimated what I was walking into.

The Marshall House had once served as a hospital during the Civil War and again during two yellow fever epidemics. Its walls had absorbed generations of grief.

At check-in, the concierge casually informed me that my room was on the floor of the ghost cat. She said I might hear her meowing at night—and possibly the sounds of children running overhead or a ball rolling across the floor. None of it sounded threatening. Honestly, it just made me more curious.

That first night, I settled in easily. Aside from the musty scent of antique wood and a creepy old chair in the corner, I felt fine. I drifted off without incident.

Then, in the middle of the night, I was jolted awake by a man's voice—right in my ear: "BOO!"

It wasn't subtle. It was loud and close, as if he were right beside me, breathing on my skin. My eyes flew open, and I saw his face: a young man in a Civil War uniform, blonde, with bulging blue eyes.

Panic surged through me. I sat bolt upright.

In hindsight, I realize how naive I was. I had assumed I'd be spared because I'm a medium. That I'd be "in the club." But that was a mistake. These weren't my spirits. I was on their turf.

I stated my boundaries aloud, clearly and firmly. He left me alone after that, but I couldn't fall back asleep. When I checked in with my guides—demanding why they'd let someone disturb me—they said, "He was just messing around. He thought it would be funny."

I did not agree.

"Fuck this," I muttered, diving under the covers. "I'm not staying here another night." I buried myself under pillows and waited out the dark, sleepless and alert.

Doors slammed in the hallway throughout the night—ghostly, disembodied bangs that matched reports from other guests. What the hell was I thinking?

By the time daylight broke, I was deeply relieved. I got up, grabbed coffee and breakfast, and headed downstairs to the parlor. I still wanted to connect with the spirits there—but on my own terms, in the safety of the sun.

In the center of the fireplace where logs would normally sit, someone had placed a massive selenite crystal. I laughed when I saw it. Everyone knew this place was haunted.

I settled into an antique chair by the window, its fabric worn smooth with age. The perfect spot to watch the sidewalk without drawing attention. Not wanting to speak aloud to the spirits, I turned instead to my usual practice: automatic writing.

I opened my journal, placed my pen to the page, introduced myself, and waited.

These are the three stories I received at The Marshall House.

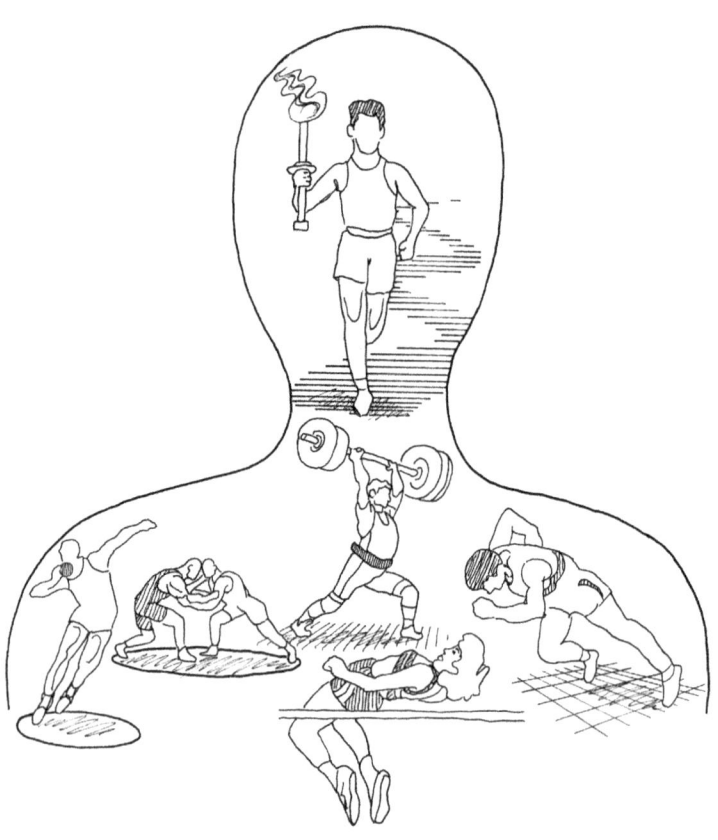

CHAPTER 15

Bonnie

Lindsay: I'm here to listen for anyone who wants to connect.

Bonnie: I'm an old person—very old. I feel hollow and light. I was frail and scared inside, like I might fall apart. Everything moves slowly and feels heavy; even just getting around takes effort. The southern heat doesn't help either. It all feels like… drudgery. I don't know what you can do, but being here like this is hard.

Lindsay: Hi, Bonnie. It's lovely to meet you. Thank you for reaching out. Give me a moment—let's see what comes through.

What I'm sensing now is a powerful, fast-moving, vibrant young man—a fit athlete, quick and fiercely competitive. This is your next life choice. Your spirit longs to run free, to move with strength and confidence. It's been waiting to feel strong again.

Your parents will be athletes—maybe even Olympic level. Both of them. Especially your mother: muscular, grounded, fiercely capable. She will nurture you with strength—in body and spirit. She knows how to support life well, and you will thrive within her care. Her womb will be your launchpad.

The Akashic Records are saying: **"Find your mother first."**

This strength you crave begins with her body. By choosing her, you'll be protected, supported, and shaped by that strength. You'll become someone who pushes limits, competes with love, and honors the body as a sacred vessel. It's beautiful.

Bonnie: I'm a man? Ha! Well… okay. I can accept that. I understand.

Lindsay: It's the embodiment that matters—your soul seeks strength, not just a specific form. Seek out the energetic imprint of that kind of mother—the one who carries power with care. That's where your next story begins.

Bonnie: Thank you. I can imagine her. I'll look for her. I truly appreciate this.

Lindsay: I'm so glad to hear that. Thank you, Bonnie.

Mourning Reflection

CHOOSING YOUR FAMILY

We often hear the phrase, "You don't choose your family." But in the Akashic Records, a different truth reveals itself again and again. While we may not choose our family's personalities, quirks, or emotional patterns, our souls absolutely choose the container—the vessel through which we enter this life.

We don't just choose a family—we choose an origin story. We choose the foundation that will shape who we're becoming.

We choose the body.

The environment.

The cells.

The privileges.

The soil our roots will grow in.

For Bonnie, that choice was clear: After a lifetime marked by frailty and exhaustion, her soul longed for strength—not just emotional or spiritual resilience, but physical vitality. She sought a vessel that could hold that new identity. The mother she now searches for is more than a caregiver—she is a force. An Olympian in body and spirit. A blueprint of power and discipline. By being born from her, Bonnie won't just be protected—she will be forged.

The strength Bonnie seeks won't just surround her; it will become her.

Sometimes we choose families not for emotional warmth, but for cellular inheritance—for the health of the womb, the length of the legs, the lung capacity. Sometimes it's about privilege—a passport, access to resources, language, or safety. Sometimes it's geography: We need to be in a specific place at a specific time. And sometimes we're in a hurry and we take the fastest route in—whoever's open, whoever can receive us.

It may not always look poetic. But it's purposeful.

If your family feels like a mismatch, it doesn't mean your soul made a mistake. Sometimes the match isn't about comfort—it's about access. Access to a body that can endure, lineage that can launch, or a doorway into the world.

This lifetime demands strength—and not just metaphorical strength, but the kind that lives in muscle, memory, and blood. You wouldn't be here if you didn't already carry it within you. Even if you don't feel strong every day, even if you're still healing from what shaped you, trust that you came prepared. You're made of lifetimes of endurance and intention.

And if nothing else, remember this:

You chose to be here.

And that, in itself, is a powerful act of courage.

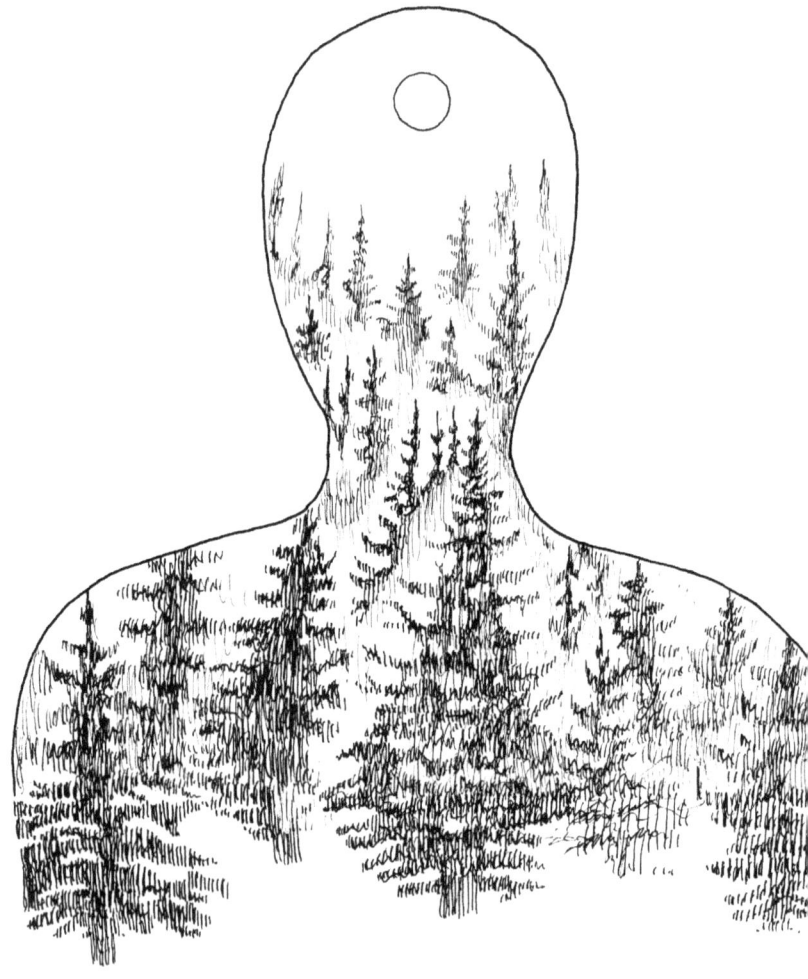

CHAPTER 16

Lieutenant Jeffries

Continuing my assistance in the parlor room, I invite another individual to come forward with their story.

"Mr. Jeffries. Lieutenant Jeffries, to be clear," a man says as I jot down his words in my notebook.

He continues, "I was speared through my chest in battle—through my ribs and out my back. I survived, but breathing was difficult from then on. I was torn between struggling to breathe to stay alive and not wanting to live anymore.

I thought it would be easier to die, and when it finally happened, I was relieved.

But my breathing caused the struggle—and my blood system. Sometimes my lungs would fill with blood. I never fully healed, but I managed to survive for a while. I was a wounded man. Breathing was hard.

I'm concerned about air quality, asthma, and similar health issues. The air is thick here in the South, and I can't imagine living in this environment—no way, no how. I wish it could be somewhere else. I want to breathe easily, without any struggle. I'm exhausted from that fight."

I greet him, "Hi, Lieutenant Jeffries. Nice to meet you. The Akashic Records are showing me a future life where trees support your lungs in healing. There's a lush, heavily wooded place that helps to clear that imprint.

When you return, consider climate change. Choose your location first—somewhere with abundant trees and a stable ecosystem. Then select the people who will be your parents. For you, it feels less about the individuals themselves. You're a self-sufficient soul with a military background—capable of navigating relationships with all kinds of people.

Your life will be respected no matter what. Let it evolve from a strong foundation in the land itself. I say this because, going forward, the Earth may not be as generous as it once was. Choose a place that has sustained clean air and healthy land for at least a hundred years. You need that kind of environment to thrive. Does that sound good?"

"Yes, sounds great. Thank you so much," the lieutenant says.

"You're so welcome."

Mourning Reflection

CHOOSING LIFE BY LOCATION

Lieutenant Jeffries's story reminded me that for some souls, the land itself is the first and most essential choice. He wasn't seeking a particular family, culture, or opportunity—he was seeking air. Trees. Breath. His soul longed for an environment that could carry life gently, where the simple act of breathing wasn't a battle.

We often think of reincarnation as a choice shaped by people or purpose. But what if, sometimes, the most sacred decision is geographic? The quality of the air. The feel of the soil. The stability of the ground beneath our feet.

This kind of choice is becoming more urgent. As climate change accelerates, wars displace millions, and ecosystems collapse, the availability of breathable, livable land is no longer guaranteed. The question is shifting—from Who will my parents be? to Where can I survive?

Where is the land still sacred? Where does nature still thrive?

In places where the Earth is honored, humanity can flourish. In places where it's stripped or poisoned, souls struggle to find rest—even in the womb.

The land is alive. Some landscapes speak directly to the soul—forests that restore, mountains that steady, waters that cleanse. A soul may feel the call of a place long before it chooses a body.

So I invite you to consider this—not just metaphysically, but practically:

If you were to start over, and the land itself was your first choice… What kind of place would you seek?

What would feel like home, not just to your body, but to your spirit?

And more importantly:

What can you do now to protect that place—for your future and for the souls yet to come?

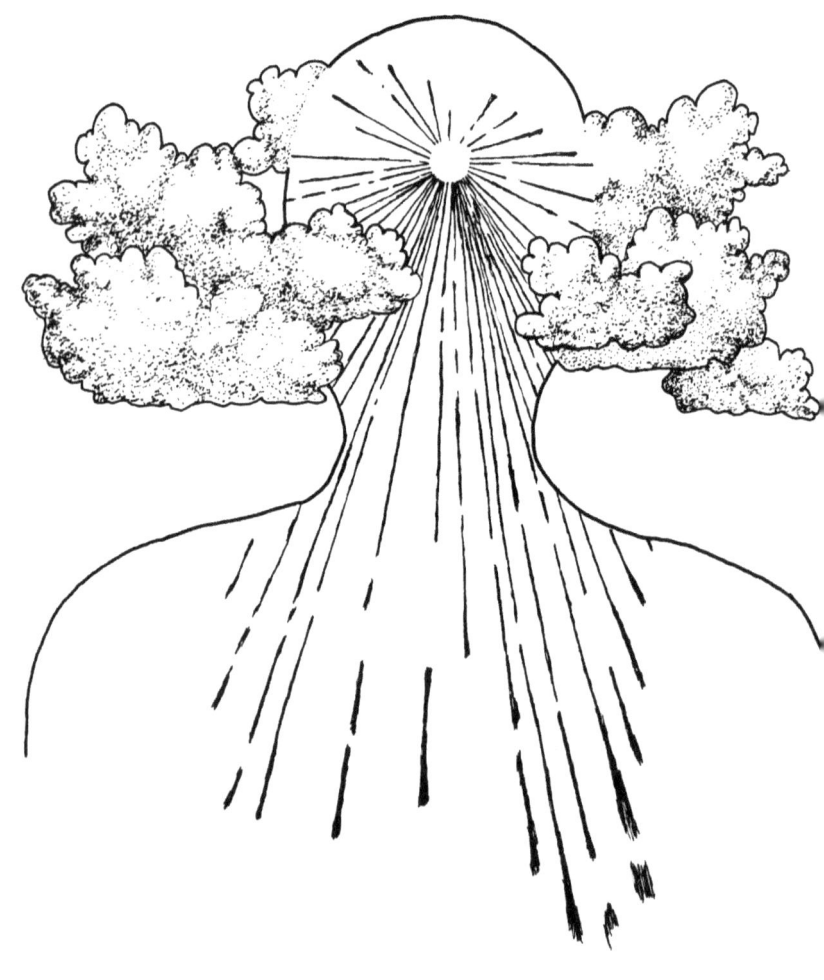

CHAPTER 17

Leonard

Shifting in the antique chair, its wood creaking beneath me, I glanced around the parlor. The air felt still—the wandering guests were gone.

Then a name surfaced from the silence: Leonard.

Leonard: I am here, just sitting around. You are a mystery to me. I can be heard clearly. This is different from usual. We try to be heard but are often feared instead. Thank you for listening to us—and to me.

Lindsay: Hi, Leonard. Yes, I'm here to listen to your stories, and when you're ready, I can offer suggestions for your next life. No pressure, of course. Go ahead.

Leonard: I died here, in a bed, quietly and peacefully. It was in a calm room. I was a sick patient. It felt peaceful here. Outside, it was chaotic. I felt I was better off in a hospital bed than out in the chaos of the world. It was a hectic place out there. I still remain in this quiet place. I stick around here.

(We are interrupted by a little boy nearby, loudly telling his mother that he saw a ghost last night.)

Leonard: I'm still a quiet person. That's it, really.

Lindsay: When were you alive here?

Leonard: In the 1870s. 1876.

Lindsay: Since you seem at peace and appear content, I wonder what I can do for you. Typically, I hear stories of more challenging passings, after which a new vision for life comes to me—one that includes healing. However, in your case, I see the sky opening up. It's as if the clouds are parting in the center, revealing light and blue skies above—an invitation to rise higher. Perhaps it's a next level.

Leonard: I'm not ready. I really like it here. Many people come by. Witnessing them in this space feels right to me. Thank you, truly.

Lindsay: Of course. It's nice to meet you, Leonard.

Leonard: Nice to meet you, too.

Mourning Reflection

THE UNKNOWN

I never experienced an invitation from the Akashic Records like that before—a call to ascend further into the sky, to reach the next level. It was intriguing and intentionally vague, perhaps more so for me than for Leonard.

What lies up there? Why venture to that place, and does the expanse of space ever truly end?

Sometimes I wonder: Is it actual death that we fear, or is it the vastness of what comes afterward? Maybe it's not fear at all; perhaps it's the overwhelming intensity of transformation and expansion that makes us uneasy.

It's comforting to be encapsulated in a body. The grounding familiarity of being on Earth—the invisible roots that connect you to the planet and to one another. Leonard is content to linger in his gentle way of existing and assisting from the other side. His clear "No, thank you" to the unknown feels relatable.

There is more happening in every moment than we can comprehend. Our human brains cannot digest it all. We try—digging into the past, replaying details—while simultaneously seeking assurance about the future, wanting to know that everything will be okay.

When the clouds parted for Leonard, the invitation to ascend felt infinitely peaceful. However, he didn't desire to move on to the next chapter. This meeting made me reflect on the different levels of life, death, the afterlife, and beyond.

This upleveling also made me wonder about how connecting with those in Spirit feels to me and how I sense their presence at different levels. Physically, I feel them slightly below me, at my level, as if they are standing next to me. More often, I sense them above me.

For example, S's presence in my life has changed over the years. When we first reconnected, I was in a guided meditative state, exploring the Underworld—a truly fascinating place, I must say. During those initial interactions, I found myself beneath the surface with them. No, it's not Hell; it's a deep realm rich with abstract visuals and powerful symbolism. Think of it like your dreams or the collective subconscious mind.

Our initial communications occurred through other intuitive artists. S informed me that they had important messages to share before reincarnating and that they were preparing to return. When we began speaking directly, without a third party, I felt their presence closely—almost as if they were sitting beside me.

As the years went by, our relationship evolved. One day, I suddenly realized that they were no longer beside me. Instead, they hovered above, softer and more refined.

When I checked in with them, S said, "I sort of graduated. I'm more of a guide to you now."

I asked, "Weren't you planning on reincarnating? It's been years. Not that I want you to go, but I'm curious—why haven't you left yet?"

They responded with a calm clarity:

"These are challenging times. I'm more effective as your guide. This is where I can be most useful—to you and to my loved ones. Someday, I'll see you again in the flesh. But not anytime soon."

Loved ones who have passed away often linger around for a while. They stay close to protect and comfort us. Eventually, they move on to a place that feels beyond our reach. Where they go always seems to be a wonderful place.

I've never asked where that is because I have a sense that I will understand when I finally arrive there. That's how Leonard's invitation to rise up into the sky felt: mysterious yet somehow familiar.

Why do we instinctively look up when we're in pain or when we seek answers? In my darkest moments, my heavy heart always lifts my gaze toward the stars. It's an innate response. Regardless of what you believe in—Heaven, angels, the cosmos, God, or the Universe—it all exists above us.

The word "Akasha" means "sky" and "all that is" in Sanskrit. The Akashic Records are an ever-present sky of wisdom. This boundless realm is not merely a collection of knowledge but a nurturing source of truth and compassion, offering a lifeline to all seekers. By remaining open and quiet enough to truly listen, we can tap into this vast field where every answer awaits.

Regardless of the strangeness, pain, or beauty of our journeys, we are reminded that there is always more to uncover, learn, and transform into. The possibilities are endless, inviting us to embrace a lifelong adventure of discovery and growth.

When the Storm Came, So Did They

With the intuitive insights I receive, I often sense what lies ahead, guiding me toward the best next steps. I especially value my ability to glimpse the future—it helps me prepare for the present.

In my mind, I keep a quiet checklist of what makes a good life: kind people, creative problem solvers, nature lovers, and builders—those who come together to form a supportive community, especially in challenging times. Like many of us, I reflect often on climate change and social unrest.

I'm from New York and have outgrown the grind—the unnecessary aggression. What I've craved for years is simple: friendly people and ease. A smile from a stranger. A "good morning." A wave, a quick chat, and *actually* knowing your neighbors.

For years, I considered California, New Mexico, Oregon, and Colorado. I traveled, researched, and followed my intuition—searching for a place that felt like home, somewhere that met all my criteria.

On my ghost road trip to Savannah, Georgia, I decided to stop in Asheville, North Carolina, on my way back to New York. A friend had recommended the city years earlier, saying I would love it, so I planned a visit over the Fourth of July.

As soon as I arrived in Asheville, everything felt right. The mountains, the vibrant energy, the genuine support among local artists—I felt welcomed and inspired. It quickly became one of my top choices.

Eventually, I narrowed it down to Asheville, Denver, or a mysterious third option I hoped would reveal itself. I was tired of overthinking and just wanted clarity.

When I asked my guides for help choosing, they simply said: "It's up to you."

Still searching for direction, I turned to the Akashic Records. I asked for symbols, feelings—anything to help me decide.

They told me that Colorado had too much air energy and not enough grounding. The elevation wasn't a match for me.

"It would feel like plastic wrap," they said. **"Suffocating."**

So that was a no.

When I asked about Asheville, the Records gave me an image of myself floating on my back in a wild, raging river. I was smiling—radiant. I'd be supported, but I'd need to ride the current.

It was a yes, but the intensity of the river stood out to me.

I understood that no place would be perfect. And since I had loved Asheville when I passed through, I returned in late September with a new lens: Could I live here?

The first apartment I toured felt perfect—almost too good to be true. A couple of days later, I signed the lease. I just had to wait for the walk-through and to get my keys on September 30 for an October 1 move-in.

I planned to return to New York to collect my things and officially move down. I was excited.

With time to kill, I booked Airbnbs nearby and stocked up on pantry food, water, a blow-up mattress, and bedsheets—my apartment starter pack until I could bring everything from New York.

To celebrate, I indulged in local favorites in the River Arts District. I got work done at Summit Coffee while waiting to check in, grabbed dinner from 12 Bones BBQ, and bought a swan candle from Marquee as a housewarming gift.

I daydreamed about settling in for fall—marveling at the mountains, breathing in crisp air, enjoying campfires and hikes, meeting new friends at coffee shops and galleries, listening to live music.

It had been gloomy and rainy for days, but I was in such a good mood, I barely noticed. The ground was squishy and saturated. The rain wouldn't quit.

I caught headlines about Hurricane Helene approaching Florida, but I didn't think much of it—Asheville felt far away.

A client from Florida messaged me, asking if I'd do an Akashic Records reading on Hurricane Helene. I'd been sharing videos of readings on YouTube, and she thought this would be helpful. But I was too focused on moving to consider it.

Later, I finally checked into my next Airbnb. My host messaged me that the space was ready, though she'd be staying a bit longer. She and her husband had planned to head to Tennessee for the weekend, but flooding in the basement had delayed her. Her husband had already left, and she would follow once conditions improved.

When I arrived, the house was framed by towering catalpa trees, like silent guardians. Everything was lush and drenched in moisture from the rain.

I felt an urge to park my car at the very top of the driveway, right in front of my private entrance. That decision would prove to be crucial.

I adored the place. Shelves of seashells and dried flowers, antique wooden furniture, a velvet couch—it felt warm, inviting, familiar. Like love had lived there.

I unpacked, made dinner, curled up in bed, and exhaled. I was tired but relieved. After a long journey of searching, it felt like I had found the beginning of home.

———

I was startled awake by the blaring smoke detector. My heart pounded as my eyes adjusted to the darkness. I rushed from the bedroom into the living room.

There was no smoke. No fire.

Unable to reach the ceiling, I grabbed a chair, climbed up, and tried to silence the alarm—but I couldn't. Frustrated, I finally removed the batteries to make it stop.

I looked around again. Nothing seemed wrong. Still shaken, I returned to the bedroom and checked the time: 6:03 a.m.

Then I heard my guides:

"Get up. Stay up. Stay alert. AccuWeather. Accurate weather."

I checked the radar.

The eye of the storm was only 88 miles away—**the hurricane was hitting us.**

My ears rang—my sign to listen.

"I'm listening," I said aloud.

"Stay up. Stay alert."

Moments later, I heard a loud CRACK, then a BOOM.

A woman screamed, *"Oh my God!"*

A massive oak tree had fallen just behind my car—missing it by mere feet.

My host called from upstairs.

"Hey there, Lindsay—we're about to become friends," she said.

A seasoned Floridian, she walked me through what to do and where to stay safe in the house.

Then she said, "Thank God you pulled your car up. How did you know to do that?!"

The storm intensified. Then the power went out.

Cell service lasted just long enough for me to call my parents and send photos of the tree behind my car. We marveled at how lucky I was, and we agreed to stay in touch.

Friends texted to check in, but halfway through replying, my messages stopped going through.

By 11 a.m., all communication went dark. No phones, no updates— only wind and rain.

I sat in the silence, braced for anything, ready to move if needed.

When the storm finally eased, Lisa came by to let me know she was heading out to check on nearby family.

Restless, I stepped outside to start clearing debris.

One by one, neighbors joined me. Families emerged, some with kids wearing helmets to protect from falling branches. Mothers, grandmothers, fathers with chainsaws.

One dad showed up with a chainsaw, a hacksaw, clippers, and a miniature rake—for the kids. Something for everyone.

In about 90 minutes, we cleared the tree behind my car and carved a path through the road. A second tree from the same yard had fallen across the other side.

As more neighbors arrived from nearby streets, we began to grasp the full scope. People were walking, biking, driving in—only to be turned around.

"The French Broad River swallowed the River Arts District," someone said.

"We're trapped. Every road is damaged, blocked by trees, or underwater. The only way in or out is by helicopter."

Not knowing the area, I stayed put, concentrating on whatever was right in front of me. Helping the neighbors calmed my anxiety and kept me grounded.

The families around me quickly became familiar. Vulnerability was enough to bring us together, and we worked side by side to get through it.

I was moved by how fast everyone stepped up—and how they welcomed me, even as a stranger.

After hauling branches for a while, my body felt sore. I went back inside the house and took a shower—the best one I've ever had. I was so exhausted that I could barely stand under the water.

As night fell, the neighborhood grew quiet. No lights, no power—

just voices, drifting from house to house.

I lit my swan candle and sat in the quiet, listening.

Though I was rattled, I felt held—hugged—by my invisible companions.

I kept replaying it: how they'd woken me with the smoke alarm.

How they had warned me. Protected me.

"Thank you so much," I whispered.

And then I went to sleep, knowing I'd wake to a very different tomorrow.

The next morning, I felt like I'd been hit by a truck. I dragged myself to the bathroom and turned the faucet—no water.

Minutes later, my host knocked on the door, her eyes glassy with tears. She asked how I was doing, then calmly explained things were much worse than we thought—the water treatment plant had been wiped out. We'd be without water for at least two weeks.

Her husband was stranded on the roof of their home in Tennessee, being airlifted food and water. She hugged me tightly. I knew I had to leave—not only for myself, but to lighten the load on her.

"I'm going to meet up with my family and keep trying to stay in touch with my husband. If you can get out of Asheville, you should try," she said.

I assessed my supplies—what would spoil, what could stretch. I counted every bottle of water, laid it all out, and felt overwhelmed. I still didn't have the keys to my apartment and couldn't reach anyone to get them. I needed a plan.

I went for a walk—our only way to gather information. With no signal or news, all we had was word of mouth and what we could see right in front of us.

Eventually, I stumbled upon my future home. To my relief, it was closer than I'd realized—and unharmed. The floodwaters had stopped just a hundred feet from the building.

Across the street, semi-trucks sat submerged, their windshield wipers eerily sweeping back and forth—though no one was inside. People wandered through the streets, phones held to the sky, hoping for a signal. There was no connection—only disbelief and nervous jokes.

Days earlier, I'd been at 12 Bones BBQ, Marquee, and Summit Coffee. Now, all three were underwater. It didn't seem real that places so full of life could vanish overnight.

I avoided the bridge, where people were gathering to watch the damage—too afraid of what I might see. But from a nearby hill, I spotted Cotton Mill Studios. Only the top of the two-story brick building was still visible. A shipping container floated past in the current.

The French Broad River had consumed everything. I didn't want to imagine what else it had taken. A chill ran up my spine at the thought.

Though the storm had passed, its destruction wasn't done. The grief was only beginning. I returned to the closest thing I had to home.

Restless and disconnected from the outside world, I turned to the one source always available to help: the Akashic Records.

I opened the Records, asking for guidance. From their perspective, I saw Asheville like a wound—muddy, raw, exposed.

"There's only one narrow way out," they told me. **"Stay where you are. You are safe. Don't go searching yet."**

My guides echoed it: **"Wait. We'll let you know when there's a way out."**

So I waited.

Two hours later, the mother from next door returned from the elementary school, where they were distributing food and water. She'd heard of one road open into South Carolina and offered to draw me a map. I handed her my journal, and she sketched the turns. "Wait until dark," she suggested, "to avoid traffic."

But my guides were firm: **"Go now. Before it gets dark."**

I packed my things, left a note and some extra water for my host, and left at 6 p.m. I felt torn and completely on edge.

The mother's directions were perfect. My exit was just five minutes away, and miraculously, none of the fallen trees blocked my path. Each had landed between houses, sparing people and property.

As I drove past gas stations, I saw the lines stretching endlessly. I was grateful I had filled my tank two days earlier.

I headed east on I-26 with no GPS, only handwritten notes in my journal. The interstate was clear of traffic—either because others had already left or hadn't heard it was open. Emergency crews had pushed trees aside to make a narrow path.

I passed bridges lined with cars waiting for fuel, towns without power, and roads washed out by the storm. Trees peeked out from beneath floodwaters. After ninety minutes, I finally got a cell signal. Texts and alerts flooded in.

I called my parents. "I'm okay! It's really bad in Asheville. I'm heading home, but I don't know where to stop."

"Just come home safely," they said. They offered to help find hotels along the way.

I kept driving. Every exit, every hotel was full. Parking lots overflowed. I'd walk in and ask, only to be turned away before finishing the question. "Sorry. Everything's booked."

Displaced people from three states were all trying to find somewhere to sleep. So I turned north on I-95 toward New York.

Driving alone at night was terrifying. Every rest stop felt unsafe. I asked my guides to help me stay alert.

"Please just get me there safely."

"Always," they said. **"We've got you."**

At 3 a.m., after five failed attempts, I finally found a hotel in Virginia. I had been on the road for ten hours. Exhausted, wired, and ready to fall apart, I slept for just four hours before continuing.

The further north I drove, the more surreal it felt. Life outside the storm zone was moving as usual. But I was still in crisis.

The road felt dangerous—not because of the storm, but because I felt invisible. Drivers cut me off, sped past. They had no idea what I'd just lived through. I felt raw, fragile, and desperate to get home.

Crossing into New Jersey, then New York, a wave of doubt hit me. I cried uncontrollably. Nowhere felt right.

I tried to talk myself down: There's no water in Asheville. Your things are in New York. It was the safer choice.

But my heart wanted to stay. I wanted to help the people who helped me—the ones who showed up. I had found community, and I left it.

"Just get home," I told myself.

When I walked in the door, my parents hugged me. I was safe. That night, I finally saw the news. The destruction was worse than I'd imagined. Grief and gratitude mixed together as I thought of my host and her neighbors.

Nothing prepares you for crisis. You move on instinct, on adrenaline. I regretted leaving but knew I had to. Staying would've meant fewer resources for the people who needed them most.

I texted my host, knowing it wouldn't go through yet—just so it would be there when it could.

In the days that followed, I broke down often. I couldn't function. I kept flashing back to the faces I'd seen. Their strength, their kindness. I sent them love, again and again.

Then something clicked. Standing in the kitchen, I realized: Everything I'd been searching for—I had found.

As climate change worsens, I've always asked: Where will people take care of each other? Where will they show up?

During that storm, I found those people. Grounded, capable, generous—even in catastrophe.

I found my place. I found my people. The living ones—with all the love and guidance from those on the other side.

Final Thoughts

Over the past five years, as I've collected and lived these stories, the world has only grown more intense. We're still feeling the impact of a global pandemic. Climate disasters are worsening. Political systems are strained, and many of us are stretched thin—mentally, emotionally, spiritually. It feels like humanity is on the brink—and it can be hard to maintain hope. Without my spiritual support systems, I don't know how I would have stayed grounded or found the strength to keep going.

This book offers only a glimpse into my experiences with mediumship and the Akashic Records. I have witnessed and supported countless stories over the years, but these particular ones stood out—they felt urgent, timely, and important to share at this moment.

I'm fascinated by human potential and how our lives fit together like pieces of a larger puzzle. Often, it's only in hindsight that we see the full picture and how everything connects. If any part of these stories feels true to you, it's worth trusting that it is.

I'll never forget the insight I got weeks before Hurricane Helene—a clear vision from the Akashic Records of myself floating on my back down a raging river, smiling. That calm, supported feeling stayed with me and helped me trust I would be okay, even when everything around me was falling apart.

I will always be grateful for the smoke alarm that woke me urgently, my guides triggering a warning moments before a tree crashed down. And the instinct that told me to park my car further up the driveway. And how all the fallen trees *narrowly* missed the cars and houses in the neighborhood.

Every detail mattered. And because I listened—because I stayed connected—I experienced something profound. It wasn't just personal. It was a glimpse into a universal relationship that's available to all of us.

Even when my physical world felt anything but safe, that deeper knowing sustained me. It reminded me that I wasn't alone and encouraged me to keep going.

The clarity and consistency of the Akashic Records—and the undeniable presence of the dead in our daily lives—are difficult to ignore. I don't share these stories to prove anything, but because they've left me in awe. Humbled. Changed.

You are a medium, too. You have a team and a support system always nearby. If you're ever lost or unsure, try listening. Those quiet nudges might lead you to something extraordinary—an experience, a truth, a guidance that changes everything.

Moving to Asheville wasn't just a relocation. It was confirmation. It showed me that my intuition was trustworthy and that the support I receive isn't limited by time or place. It's with me always—and it's with you too.

Mediumship bridges Heaven and Earth, offering an unconditional line of connection no matter where we are in life. Looking back, I see the grief—but right beside it, there's a deep, steady love. Even in my most challenging moments, that love was always present, patiently waiting for me to find it. It's waiting for you, too, if you let it in.

ABOUT THE ARTIST

Andy Vible is an American artist and musician whose work blends mythology, popular culture, and everyday objects into surreal, narrative-driven imagery. He works across sculpture, collage, painting, drawing, murals, and printmaking, and has exhibited nationally. He lives and works in Wilmington, Delaware.

ABOUT THE AUTHOR

Lindsay Mann is a medium, meditation teacher, Reiki Master, and intuitive artist. Before dedicating herself to spiritual work, she worked as a fashion designer in New York. Now based in the Blue Ridge Mountains, she writes and teaches to help others find clarity, insight, and spiritual connection. She is the author of *Beyond Love*, *30 Questions to Ask the Akashic Records to Change the World*, and *Soul Garden*.

www.ingramcontent.com/pod-product-compliance
Lightning Source LLC
Chambersburg PA
CBHW051530120626
46551CB00012B/1161